7 95

Connie Gowen
455 Pebble Beach Pl.
Fullerton, CA 92635

D0032589

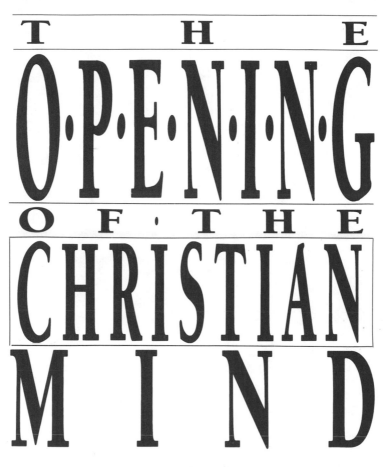

THE O·P·E·N·I·N·G OF·THE CHRISTIAN MIND

Taking Every Thought
Captive to Christ

DAVID W. GILL

Foreword by Earl F. Palmer

INTERVARSITY PRESS
DOWNERS GROVE, ILLINOIS 60515

©1989 by David W. Gill

All rights reserved. No part of this book may be reproduced in any form without written permission from InterVarsity Press, P.O. Box 1400, Downers Grove, Illinois 60515.

InterVarsity Press is the book-publishing division of InterVarsity Christian Fellowship, a student movement active on campus at hundreds of universities, colleges and schools of nursing. For information about local and regional activities, write Public Relations Dept., InterVarsity Christian Fellowship, 6400 Schroeder Rd., P.O. Box 7895, Madison, WI 53707-7895.

Distributed in Canada through InterVarsity Press, 860 Denison St., Unit 3, Markham, Ontario L3R 4H1, Canada.

All Scripture quotations, unless otherwise indicated, are from the Holy Bible, New International Version. Copyright © 1973, 1978, International Bible Society. Used by permission of Zondervan Bible Publishers.

ISBN 0-8308-1279-2

Printed in the United States of America ⊗

Library of Congress Cataloging-in-Publication Data

Gill, David W., 1946-
   The opening of the Christian mind.

   Bibliography: p.
   1. Christian life—1960-   .   2. Faith and reason.
I. Title.
BV4509.5.G478   1989   248.8'34   89-1724
ISBN 0-8308-1279-2

17	16	15	14	13	12	11	10	9	8	7	6	5	4	3	2	1
99	98	97	96	95	94	93	92	91	90	89						

For
my fellow Christians
past, present and future
at my alma mater,
the University of California,
Berkeley

248.834
G4750
1989 c.2

Foreword _____ 9

Preface _____ 13

1: THE IDEA OF A CHRISTIAN MIND _____ 19

2: THE CHALLENGE OF A TECHNO-PLURALISTIC WORLD _____ 33

3: THE STRENGTH AND WEAKNESS OF TODAY'S UNIVERSITY _____ 47

4: SIX MARKS OF A CHRISTIAN MIND _____ 63

5: THE CHRISTIAN MIND AT WORK _____ 79

6: ENVIRONMENTAL REQUIREMENTS FOR CHRISTIAN MINDS _____ 91

7: STUDY LIST: THE CHRISTIAN MIND CURRICULUM _____ 103

8: STRATEGIES FOR BUILDING A CHRISTIAN MIND _____ 113

9: GRADUATION REQUIREMENTS: WHAT IT TAKES
   TO SALT THE EARTH _____ 129

Bibliography _____ 139

Foreword

The Opening of the Christian Mind is a book that needed to be written. Much more than a book, it is the journal of a pioneer. David Gill has been living this story since his undergraduate days at the University of California, Berkeley, and his book invites us to share his excitement and the importance of his vision.

David Gill and I first met each other during the ideologically and politically stormy years of the mid-seventies. Since 1970 I have been the pastor of First Presbyterian Church of Berkeley, just two blocks from the entrance to the university campus. Here in Berkeley an atmosphere of isolation characterized the years following the Vietnam War and the explosive campus protests of the sixties. Suspicion and disillusionment with the formal structures of American society led many to attempt a conscious disconnection from those structures and the expectations of such established institutions as government, the university, organized churches, the business culture and the traditional family.

A subculture of alienated, rootless people (very different from the hoboes of earlier times) chose isolation as a dominant lifestyle. They expressed this isolation in various ways, some escapist, some apathetic, some aggressively radical. Because our culture places such a high premium on personal freedom and, at the same time, provides a generous social welfare safety net, it was not only possible but relatively painless for many young Americans to "drop out" and live on the margins of our society without much responsibility or purpose in life.

But this isolated, alienated lifestyle was becoming the experience of another group. Although their mode of dress and visible lifestyle did not dramatize this choice, many mainstream, hardworking, tax-paying Americans began living and working from day to day with no more sense of a reason for daily life, and with no more grand objectives and goals, than their more colorful counterparts living in the park, the car or the commune. Life and work without significance, meaning, purpose and mission beyond the most basic impulses and instincts has become the fate of an isolated, disconnected people.

In this ideological climate my church has been trying evangelistically, prophetically, and educationally to assist Christians in discovering a profound mission as disciples of Jesus Christ both in the university and the workplace. In the early seventies several of us in the Christian community in Berkeley discovered that we shared some common goals along these lines. Our first united efforts were in the form of study courses sponsored by what we called The Crucible. These were our first tentative efforts to teach courses directed toward the laity with the definite goal of creating a new kind of lay Christian awareness. Our purpose was to stir up Christians to a sense of the exciting relevance of the Gospel of Jesus Christ for the secular work of our hands and minds.

In this setting, David Gill was for us a pacesetter, but his vision was even more dramatic and far-reaching than what the informal Crucible courses could offer. David dreamed of a graduate school in Berkeley that would exclusively commit itself to the vision of enabling lay Christians to actively study the Christian faith in such a way that Jesus Christ would truly reign over all of life, including the work of their hands and minds. David's vision was to create a fellowship of Christians which would be transdenominational, evangelical, biblically serious and deeply committed to the goal of bringing biblical Christianity into the very places where we work each day. His idea was that we should start a school for laity, not a seminary (since we already have many fine seminaries to train pastors). He wanted this school to be a thoughtful evangelical presence in Berkeley, in constructive relation to both the University of California and the seminaries of the Graduate Theological Union.

David Gill's vision soon took hold of the rest of us. When David and I discovered that we shared this vision and that we both had been deeply influenced by the ministry of Regent College in Vancouver, British Columbia (a college with aims similar to those of our New College Berkeley), we became natural partners in the dream (though I have always been the junior partner in this project!). While David worked on his Ph.D. at the University of Southern California, we began to exchange letters and meet together to dream. We began to describe our goal as "a new college in Berkeley."

By the end of 1976, out of the dozens of people with whom we shared this vision and from whom we received almost unanimous encouragement, a small steering committee composed of David and myself, Walter and Virginia Hearn, Sharon Gallagher, Bev Schmidt, Robert Schoon, Cal Farnham, Bob Baylis and Craig Anderson came together to make the school a reality with God's help. Kent Meads, Steve Phillips, Jim Barringer, Minor Schmidt, Joan Anderson and many others joined in helping our project as it became a reality, officially founded on April 7, 1977. After serving as our project director for just over two years, in the fall of 1979 David became our first dean and Ward Gasque arrived from Regent College to be our first president.

Now, more than a decade later, David Gill is our president and we have passed our ten-year mark. God has blessed our vision because it is sound and biblical and our cause is urgent. It is the vision of Christ at the center of the city, not relegated to the edge; it is the vision of lives, minds, hearts and hands in the service of the Lord; it is the vision of men and women teamed together in Christian community, seeking to live with Jesus Christ as the Lord of all of life.

This vision of theological relevance for Christian men and women in our world must begin with our "taking captive every thought to the obedience of Christ." Thus we must begin with the minds and hearts of ordinary Christians. *The Opening of the Christian Mind* is a book about minds that are no longer disconnected and isolated but rather profoundly connected and integrated with the grand design and purpose of the God who made our minds. David Gill's study is a very important building block for the journey of each person, young or old, who dares to recognize and then trust the faithfulness and grace of God that welds not only our thinking but the whole created order.

Earl F. Palmer
Senior Pastor
First Presbyterian Church of Berkeley

Preface

Among the most important of my parents' gifts to me was the deep conviction that Jesus Christ is Lord of the whole of life, including the whole of *my* life. The Christian life is the great adventure of exploring what that leadership means.

The Opening of the Christian Mind is a report on some central aspects of that adventure of discipleship as I have come to understand it. By the term *Christian mind* I refer to the giving of our minds to Jesus the Lord (and not practicing a mindless Christianity having to do only with our emotions or tradition). Too often Christians check their minds at the door with their coats when they enter the church . . . and worse, check their Christianity at the door when they enter the university or business office. This book is a manifesto for being "transformed by the renewing of your mind" (Rom 12:2).

Obviously, my title recalls *The Closing of the American Mind*, the 1987 best seller by Allan Bloom. Pretending to be open, the American mind has become empty and, in reality, closed. The typical Christian mind is certainly not empty, but it is underdeveloped and undervalued. Our

Christian minds have too often been fearful, insecure and closed. My call is first of all to open the Christian mind toward God, inviting him to expand, invigorate and shape our thinking toward the mind of Christ. I do think, however, that such a movement will also bring with it greater openness to and respect for other people, their knowledge, wisdom and opinions.

Let me also warn (reassure?) you that *The Opening of the Christian Mind* is not a manifesto for intellectualism in any sense. It is crucial that a Christian mind be properly located in a richly textured life of worship, evangelism, friendship, mutual care and all other aspects of the Christian life. We do not need any more dry, irrelevant armchair-Christian intellectuals!

The Opening of the Christian Mind is written primarily with university students and working graduates in mind. But my message is as appropriate for young children and non-university people as it is for the highly educated.

My experience as a student, especially as an undergraduate at the University of California at Berkeley in the mid and late sixties, nurtured an intense and persistent desire for a truly Christian mind. On the one hand, I was a student in one of the finest history departments in America. On the other hand, I was a convinced, practicing Christian. My Bible, family and church insisted that Jesus was active today as always in human history. But my history professors never so much as mentioned Jesus as a factor in history. How could this gap be bridged? How could I develop a *Christian* historical mind? Had anyone else ever thought about this?

On my own I discovered that people like Herbert Butterfield, Christopher Dawson, Eric Voegelin and John Warwick Montgomery had, in fact, thought and written about a Christian view of history. Emboldened by their writings, and more generally by the creative work of Francis Schaeffer, I wrote and defended an M.A. thesis on "Contemporary Christian Philosophies of History: The Problem of God's Role in Human History" at San Francisco State University. For four years I taught high school and junior high history, adding a second set of integrative questions to address two essential parts of my life: How could I approach public-school teaching as a *Christian* educator?

Far from being discouraged, and despite my naiveté and isolation, my efforts were rewarded with progressive understanding. I was thoroughly convinced that it was not only biblically mandated but really possible for Christians studying in secular universities and working in a pluralistic world to develop unified Christian perspectives on their fields—and then to think, work and live as veritable salt and light in the midst of that world. Unquestionably this is a lifelong task, not a fixed accomplishment, but it is a meaningful, often joyful task rather than a burden.

Scripture does not prepare Christians for isolated individualism, no matter how much the culture affirms it. I began early on to look for community or institutional support for my quest. But my family and church were unable to help much because I was the only historian—and public school-teacher—among them. Their integrative focus, insofar as it existed, was necessarily on other fields. Bible schools and Christian colleges did not seem to be addressing integrative questions and were, additionally, located (symbolically?) far from the world where I studied and worked. Campus Christian groups were (and, for the most part, still are) not much interested in notions of a Christian mind (a choice which continues to distress me whenever I think of the opportunities for Christians on campus). Theological seminaries, appropriately and necessarily, were focused on training pastors, not integrating lay Christian minds. One notable flicker of light came when I discovered and joined the Conference on Faith and History, a fellowship of several hundred Christian historians in North America which holds annual conferences and publishes a journal. But I yearned for something more.

In February 1970 I wrote to Francis Schaeffer urging him to start a Berkeley chapter of his L'Abri fellowship. His response was that the idea and location were right but that he was not the one to do it. In my living room in 1972, nine kindred spirits helped me give birth to a study group we called "The Crucible: A Forum for Radical Christian Studies." We operated a small library and offered various courses and workshops on or near the Berkeley campus. However the academic level at which we were able to work was inadequate, especially by comparison to our students' training in the university and its professional and graduate schools. We were offering appetizers and dessert while the university gave the main course! Thousands upon thousands of Christians were submitting to years of rigorous, demanding study in their various fields. How could we provide equally rigorous and excellent Christian integrative studies helping our fellow disciples toward Christian minds?

After paying my dues in a Ph.D. program at the University of Southern California, I and a few friends, inspired by the Canadian examples of Regent College (at the University of British Columbia) and the Institute for Christian Studies (at the University of Toronto), founded New College Berkeley on April 7, 1977, as a graduate school of Christian studies for the laity. The message of *The Opening of the Christian Mind* has been heard and acted upon by many hundreds, if not thousands, of people associated with New College Berkeley over the past ten years. Our ideals have been imperfectly realized, of course, and our plans and thinking continue to grow and get modified in various ways. But the vision is very much alive, not least among our alumni, and this book is in large part a product of the first decade of New College Berkeley.

I owe a great deal to Harry Blamires's *The Christian Mind*, Charles Habib Malik's *A Christian Critique of the University* and many other books on aspects of the Christian mind. Perhaps less obvious is the rootage of *The Opening of the Christian Mind* in John Henry Cardinal Newman's *The Idea of a University*. My idea (certainly not original with me) is in general accord with what Newman wished to see as the fruit of college and university education: unified Christian minds. Tactically, however, my idea is geared to a pluralistic world in which (according to one study) at least eighty per cent of all Christians are educated in secular colleges and universities. My institutional suggestions, while daunting enough, are thus less ambitious than fully reclaiming the great universities of our time or starting new ones.

As I suggested earlier, my first intellectual and spiritual debt is to my parents. From my father I learned the courage and tenacity to pursue any question with confidence in the truth and power of holy Scripture. From my mother I learned the joyful freedom of sharing my challenges and discoveries with others. My debts to other writers and thinkers such as Jacques Ellul and Joseph Pieper will be apparent in the text and notes. I owe a special debt to the Regent College community, especially W. Ward Gasque, who served with energy and distinction as NCB's first president, 1979-82. Many student groups on campuses too numerous to list have heard and commented on the material in this book. Various groups of Christians in different professions have similarly given their attention to these ideas at various conferences and symposia. At an annual meeting of the Western Region of the American Academy of Religion I was invited to describe "Institutional Obstetrics: The Birth of New College Berkeley" for my academic colleagues.

Most of all, of course, I am indebted to the board, faculty, staff, students and alumni of New College Berkeley. Of longest duration this refers to a fellow Cal alumnus in whose heart the same vision burns: Earl Palmer, senior pastor of First Presbyterian Church of Berkeley and my original co-conspirator in the NCB Project. Joan Anderson, Bernard Adeney, Bill Dyrness, Chris Sillerud, Frank Andersen, Rich Benner, Virginia Hearn, Craig Anderson, Fred Vann, Jim Barringer, Steve Phillips, Marilyn Shaver, Sharon Gallagher . . . this is only the beginning of the list of NCB stalwarts over the years to whom I am grateful.

Sustained by the gemütlichkeit of the Evangelische Freikirchliche Gemeinde on Holzstrasze, I managed to draft *The Opening of the Christian Mind* during two delightful summer months in Munich at the tail end of my 1984-85 sabbatical in Europe. Jim Sire and Marty Stewart both made helpful suggestions after reading the whole manuscript. Revisions were finally possible, thanks to Betty and Will DeMont and their family who let me hide out in their Ware House at Bodega Bay.

THE IDEA
OF A
CHRISTIAN
•MIND•
1

E PISODE ONE: *"No, David. You just don't understand. That is not where* students are at. They're not asking those kinds of questions. They're not ready for what you are talking about!"

The campus minister was adamant, giving me a response I had heard too many times from the professionals and experts. This time, however, I could wait no longer for his approval and co-sponsorship of my plan. With three other colleagues, I organized a two-day conference at my alma mater, the University of California, Berkeley, on "Thinking Christianly in Today's University." We hoped for two hundred to attend. Three hundred seventy-five showed up!

Episode Two: "It can't work that way. Doctors are too busy. In any case they won't attend a conference with nurses. Good luck!"

We were planning our first symposium on integrating Christian faith

with work in the health-care professions, and few believed we could pull
it off. We hoped for one hundred to attend. Three hundred twenty-five
doctors, nurses, dentists, medical students and nursing students
showed up!

The fact is that most Christians do have a deep hunger to relate their
faith to their thinking and living, their studies and then their work. But
often this is not articulated clearly or forcefully. In that respect my
ministerial friend was correct: students don't always vocalize their questions. But authentic biblical faith draws and drives us toward unified,
holistic discipleship. Heart trust yearns for brain trust—a responsible
mind being developed in the midst of responsible community—as its
companion. Small group and personal piety leads to marketplace faithfulness and to a Christian mind, or a kind of spiritual and intellectual
schizophrenia eats away at our personal wholeness and health.

I found myself hungering for a Christian way of thinking about my
life and studies even as a teenager. Still more in my undergraduate
college days and since, I have been drawn in this direction. In giving
hundreds of lectures, talks and discussions on university campuses and
among church groups over the past fifteen years or more, I have yet to
find any genuine disinterest in the kinds of ideas presented in this
book (except by a handful of professional Christian leaders whose
notions of what's good for "their people" are, on this subject, unbiblical
and condescending).[1]

To accompany us on our exploration of the Christian mind, I want
to introduce four friends of mine who will reappear in each of the
following chapters. We will need to ask (at almost every turn) what all
of this discussion means in practical terms for real people.[2]

Ellen is forty-five years old, married with two teenage children. She
lives in the suburbs and commutes each day to the financial district
where she is a vice president in charge of housing loans for one of the
largest banks in the world. Ellen graduated from a highly regarded
Christian liberal arts college in California and is an active member of
a medium-size conservative evangelical church in her suburb.

Stan is thirty-four, single and an electronics whiz at a fast-growing computer software firm in the Silicon Valley. He lives with two other Christian men; all three attend a large fundamentalist Bible church. Stan remains close to his parents, who managed to put him through Stanford by working long hours in the neighborhood grocery store they started after immigrating from Hong Kong thirty-five years ago.

Bill is twenty-six, married and proud father of an infant daughter. In six months his medical training will be finished and he will begin his M.D. practice somewhere. Educational loans from the U. C. San Francisco medical school totaling more than $30,000 hang over his head, but he has been a brilliant student and his career prospects look great. Bill attends a charismatic Episcopal church in the city.

Debbie is nineteen, single and a sophomore at Cal State University. She lives with her mother and three younger siblings ten miles from campus. They attend Mt. Zion Missionary Baptist, a small but vibrant inner-city church. Debbie has always been a solid student but is uncertain about her career direction. She is inclined to declare an English major and plan on a high-school teaching career, but she sometimes thinks that a career as an attorney might be a better choice.

I wish I also had the space to bring along Ed (a retired businessman), Lynn (a career homemaker, mother, Sunday-school teacher and neighborhood missionary), Donna (a starving artist with a lot of talent), Harry (CEO of a Fortune 500 company), James (a discontented mail carrier with a master's degree who wishes he could find a better career) and others. But I don't think it will be too difficult to figure out what developing a Christian mind means for them after reading about my four main passengers.

So let's begin the journey.

Thinking about Thinking

One of the most distinctive characteristics of human existence is that we are capable of mental reflection and thought. We are capable of self-transcendence (thinking about ourselves) through the use of our minds. We are not bound to a mechanical, unreflective obedience to instinct or conditioning. Rather, we can think about our actions and, still more remarkable, decide to go against our instincts or appetites. We are capable of amazing self-discipline, sacrifice, exertion and even heroism in the face of various challenges. This is due in large part to the fact that we have been created with minds that can reflect and choose. We can transcend nature and culture; we do not always submit passively to our situations.

Many philosophers have celebrated reason—the exercise of logical, cognitive thought—as the highest faculty of human beings and therefore the most important to be developed in the quest for a full human life. Still others have emphasized human volition—the capacity to will and to choose. A third human quality, with its own proponents hailing it as definitive in importance, is feeling or aesthetic sensitivity. To these three (reason, will, feeling) correspond the True, the Good and the Beautiful in classical philosophy. More recently, Immanuel Kant (1724-1804) wrote his three monumental Critiques of Pure Reason, Practical Reason and Judgment—again in correspondence to the three components described above.

It is easy to see how various Christian groups, past and present, have given greater stress to one or another of these components in their views of discipleship. A Christian mind, however, includes all of these factors. I advocate a holistic commitment of the activities going on in our heads to Jesus Christ as Lord. This includes what we have traditionally called our heart. I want to encourage a heart for the Lord. But—surprise!—your heart (in the biblical sense) is in your brain, not in that pump in your chest.

Reason, will and aesthetic judgment (or feeling) may be separable in theory and for analytical purposes, but in life they form a rich, interacting (if not integrated), complex whole. Our minds operate at many different speeds, at different levels, as we encounter different situations. We are evidently capable of tolerating a certain degree of chaos and even contradiction in our minds. Thus, our minds may be vigorously exercised in mastering some technical procedure or in confronting some business challenge; but this may remain uncoordinated with our knowledge of ecological factors or religious values. Or we may choose and carry out a course of action that contradicts our reason or our deepest sense of what is beautiful, fitting and true.

Part of building a Christian mind will mean developing each part of our minds into a servant of God; our task will also be to integrate these components into a coherent whole. There is, and always will be, a great deal of paradox and mystery to the life we live. We can marvel and rejoice in this complexity and richness. But the paradox and mystery of which I speak is not to be equated with the chaos and contradiction of a fragmented, half-developed mind, too lazy or distracted to work toward wholeness and integration.

The problem of the fragmented, half-developed mind owes its origins to many factors, some of which will be discussed in the following chapters. Human beings are under awesome stress in modern life and are, at the same time, deprived of many traditional sources of support for the development and deployment of Christian minds. The sheer speed and the overwhelming volume of information to be mastered, the competitiveness of the university, workplace and marketplace—these take their toll on us and keep us from grasping the whole of life. Instead we focus on the development of the part of life that is most urgent, and come home exhausted to slump in front of the television or into bed after a day at school or work.

It is the burden of this book that Christians ought to and can resist and overcome this fragmentation and begin developing healthy, integrated, whole minds under the leadership of Jesus Christ their Lord. Christians and non-Christians alike, we may invest thousands of dollars and years of our lives developing legal minds, business minds, medical minds, physics minds or computer minds. In our spare time we may nurture tennis minds, home electronics minds or automobile minds. Here you will find no diatribe against law, medicine, tennis or automobiles, however! But in all of its activities and fields, the mind must be submitted to the unity of the mind of Christ.

But *why* is a Christian mind essential for all disciples? Let's clarify this question before we plunge into a more detailed study of this challenge and seek to find a viable solution to it.

The Argument from Above

Decisive (though not exclusive) in the question of seeking a fully Christian mind is the argument from above, that is, the call and command of the Word of God. We find that we are both invited and obligated by Jesus and Scripture to carry out this adventure. Those well-meaning Christians who have worried about and warned against education, learning and the exercise of the intellect have good reason! But nowhere does the biblical revelation tell us that the answer is mindless or thoughtless discipleship. The proper response to the misuse, deformity, pride, arrogance and error of the mind is not disuse but redemption and renewal. God created, and is redeeming, whole persons—body, soul and spirit—not disembodied souls or mindless spirits. The Word of God judges and rejects sin and untruth, not the errant, mistaken sinner per se, nor the process of thinking.

The place for us to begin is with the Great Commandment given by our Lord both as a summary of the Law and Prophets (Mt 22:37-40; Mk 12:29-31) and as a summary of the way of eternal life (Lk 10:27), making it extraordinarily important for all disciples. "Love the Lord your God with all your heart and with all your soul and with all your mind and with all your strength" (Mk 12:30). This quotation from the *shema* (Deut 6:5) is notable partly because in the New Testament it *adds* the term *mind* to heart, soul, and strength given in Deuteronomy. The term *heart* had, by Jesus' time, lost its original holistic connotation of thinking as well as feeling, willing, deciding. To make perfectly certain that the mind was included in discipleship, Jesus added a term in the quotation.[3] Love God with your mind, not without it!

Our Lord both taught and exemplified a Christian mind filled with truth that sets people free. With marvelous pedagogy he shaped his disciples' minds not only about doctrine or the afterlife but about marriage, singleness, money, health, peace, justice and other components of human thinking and living. As disciples of this Jesus Christ we must work at learning how to love God with our minds. It's a command. We must continually ask how the partial and relative truths of our studies relate to *the* Truth in Jesus Christ. How can we subsume our partial devotion to a given field or problem within our absolute devotion to loving God with our minds?

The apostle Paul elaborated and explained the call to a Christian mind in unmistakable fashion. Negatively, Paul inveighed against the absence of a spiritual, Christian mind. "The man without the Spirit does not accept the things that come from the Spirit of God, for they are foolishness to him, and he cannot understand them, because they are spiritually discerned" (1 Cor 2:14). It is possible, Paul says, to have minds that are hardened, veiled, blinded, alienated, hostile, inflated and corrupted (see 2 Cor 3:14; 4:4; Col 1:21; 2:18; 1 Tim 6:5; 2 Tim 3:8). In fact, professing *Christians* sometimes display these very characteristics! These are not just attributes of non-Christians, according to Paul.

But Paul's solution is not rejection of the mind, anymore than it is continued conformity to the status quo. "See to it that no one takes you captive by hollow and deceptive philosophy, which depends on human tradition and the basic principles of this world rather than on Christ." There *is* a way of thinking that is according to Christ which is different from the traditional way. "Be transformed by the renewing of your mind" (Rom 12:2). "Let this mind be in you, which was also in Christ Jesus" (Phil 2:5 KJV). "Set your minds on things above" (Col 3:2). "We demolish arguments and every pretension that sets itself up against the knowledge of God, and we take captive every thought to make it obedient to Christ" (2 Cor 10:5). In Jesus Christ are "hidden all the treasures of wisdom and knowledge" (Col 2:3).

Our challenge could hardly be stated more clearly: it is essential to resist seduction and captivity to the way of thinking (or not-thinking) of the world around us. All knowledge and wisdom are rooted in and centered upon Jesus Christ, though it is to a certain extent hidden and not always immediately obvious. The challenge to develop a renewed mind, the mind of Christ, requires the Spirit of God on the one hand, and our aggressive complicity in "taking captive every thought," on the other.

Actually, the whole of Scripture supports this quest and voices this challenge. Many will recall the warnings of the Preacher of Ecclesiastes:

"For with much wisdom comes much sorrow; the more knowledge, the more grief" (Eccles 1:18). But remember also that this assessment of vanity, futility and emptiness relates to a life under the sun, a life limited to an immanent, this-worldly horizon. In stark contrast is the call of Proverbs to "choose . . . instruction instead of silver, knowledge rather than choice gold, for wisdom is more precious than rubies, and nothing you desire can compare with her" (Prov 8:10-11). The difference in these quotations from the wisdom literature is that, in the latter case, "The fear of the LORD is the beginning of wisdom, and knowledge of the Holy One is understanding" (Prov 9:10).

The apostle Peter might be expected, as a fisherman, to be impatient with talk of a Christian mind, but such is not the case. "Prepare your minds for action" (1 Pet 1:13). "Arm yourselves . . . with the same mind" as Christ (1 Pet 4:1 KJV).[4] These statements from Jesus, Paul, Peter, Ecclesiastes and Proverbs are just samples. The evidence throughout the Bible, both in specific texts and overarching themes, is overwhelming and consistent: God calls us away from conformity to the life of the mind around us and toward a new way of thinking.

As Christians we are not called merely to a simple repudiation of error but to a positive seizing and taking captive of all knowledge from any source into and under the lordship of Jesus Christ. The Bible illustrates as well as commands this process. Ideas and institutions from the world surrounding the people of God are taken captive, purged of error, remolded and filled with new significance in subordination to the truth and ways of God. Paul's ethical teaching, for example, incorporates elements of Stoic household codes but only by way of radically renewing, reforming and fulfilling them in the light of Christ.[5] Peter's ethical teaching incorporates elements of classical Greek ethics but, again, only in subordination to the faith, hope and love of Jesus Christ.

In short, the Bible has a great deal to say about our subject, about thinking, wisdom, learning, instruction and other affairs of the mind. Scripture reveals the essential aspects of Truth, Goodness and Beauty and locates them in relation to the God we know in Jesus Christ. This core material does not, however, remain abstract or unapplied. Rather, it is elaborated, illustrated and applied with great frequency and brilliant illumination to subjects such as money, property, law, justice, politics, health care, psychology, social work and the other constituent elements, institutions and forces in human history.

Let me say it bluntly and boldly: *There is no legitimate field of study or work which will fail to be illuminated by the Word of God.* A corollary which I think is equally true: *If a field of study or work is found, after due effort, to be impossible to locate under the lordship of Jesus Christ, the burden of proof is on us to demonstrate why we should continue in that field.*

My campus-minister friend, whose comments opened this chapter, deprives his students of the challenge to develop Christian minds—in disobedience to the clear message of Scripture. If his younger charges are not (as he says) asking those questions, then *he* should be articulating them. Developing a Christian mind is not based first of all on our felt needs or questions (arguments from below)—it is always primarily a matter of God's questions to us (from above).

In its admonition to us to develop our minds, the Bible confronts us with both a command and a promise. As a command (Love God with all your mind), it is inescapably obvious that we must respond in obedience. Disobedience here is no less serious than any other occasions of disobedience to God's commands, and it brings with it a kind of death to the mind and soul as it separates us from God. What is perhaps less obvious is the fact that God's commands are always, paradoxically, his promises. It is not merely that we *must* love God with our minds but that we *may* do so. We are confronted with a gracious invitation, a new possibility, an extraordinary adventure of knowing the Truth itself, of having the very mind of Christ in us. Within his command, God invites us to probe the sources of knowledge and understanding, to look into the mystery of our existence where we will discover a Truth that is vibrant and fully alive and which brings degrees of meaning, joy and freedom unavailable on any other path.

Developing a Christian mind turns out to be not merely *obeying* God with all our mind—but *loving* God with all our mind.

The Arguments from Below

For a disciple of Jesus Christ, the preceding argument from above (from God's revealed Word in Scripture) is sufficient and decisive. But it is also valuable to reflect on the perspective from below. Let us consider some arguments in favor of developing a unified Christian mind that are based on personal and social existence. These arguments are based on what we judge to be humanly better or worse, more meaningful or less meaningful personal experience, and socially healthy or sick, productive or destructive patterns of thought and life. In rough outline, at least, these kinds of arguments are made by philosophers, psychologists and sociologists whether Christian or not. For Christians, however, they acquire additional force if they can be located in positive relation to the Word of God.

Beginning with personal life, then, the ancient Greek philosopher Socrates was probably correct that the unexamined life is not worth living. As I argued earlier, one of the major distinctive characteristics of human existence is our capacity to think, to reflect on our life, weighing and evaluating it, modifying our ideas and patterns of life. Thus, we might conclude, it is subhuman merely to drift along, unreflectively surrendering to external forces and conditions, implicitly agreeing to be the plaything of outside forces.

If the idea of subhuman existence does not bother you, consider the contrast between meaningfulness and meaninglessness. Meaning in life—the sense of value, purpose, significance and direction—is inextricably related to the way we think. If we do not think well, we are unlikely to have a very strong sense of personal meaning and worth. To be sure, there remains a kind of meaning which can be derived from participation in a value-laden group, like a terrorist, revolutionary or fanatical movement. On closer examination, though, deriving all of one's meaning and value from being a cog in some machine indicates an absence of real, individual meaning and value. I have my doubts about a life that has no perceptible value except as being fodder in a group's cannon.

It is also a truism that the way we act is related to the way we think.

An old translation of Proverbs 23:7 says, "As a man thinketh, so is he." (This is a little more persuasive than "You are what you eat," an anonymous proverb that didn't make it into Holy Writ!) If our thinking is sloppy and shallow, our actions in life will probably display the same character. If our minds are fragmented and disjointed, our life may be the same. If your thinking is full of errors, look out for your actions!

In short, developing a unified, integrated mind is in our personal interest because of the promise it holds for richly and fully human life that is meaningful, coherent and liveable. I further submit that the best way to develop such a mind is by making Jesus Christ the Lord and center of all our thinking.

I want to explore briefly a final set of considerations from below, which are of a social and interpersonal nature. So far, I have argued that God wants you to develop a Christian mind and that it is in your personal interest to do so. What I now want to suggest is that it is in your neighbor's interest and society's interest as well. A business entrepreneur who develops habits of holistic, unified thinking, may well leave society, neighbors and the next generation much better off; he or she would be inclined to consider environmental impact, long-term consequences, and so on—not just a short-term marketing strategy aiming at maximum profits. Best of all, of course, would be a self-consciously *Christian* business person who would have the values and perspectives of the earth's creator and redeemer at the heart of such holistic considerations.

It is also a fact that unthinking or fragmented individuals are more susceptible to degrading and destructive manipulation by advertisers, propagandists and demagogues. A good preventive against the rise of authoritarianism, totalitarianism and other forms of manipulation is the development and nurture of individual men and women having coherent world views on the basis of which events, trends and people can be evaluated. Having a unified Christian mind, among other things, provides us with a sort of measuring stick to use in evaluating the ideas and phenomena which bombard us. No Christian mind, no measuring stick—chaos and uncertainty come instead.

In very different ways, three recent best sellers have stressed the social importance of citizens with broader (and better) education, deeper moral sensitivity and renewed spiritual and religious life. *Habits of the Heart* by Robert N. Bellah et al, *The Closing of the American Mind* by Allan Bloom and *Cultural Literacy* by E. D. Hirsch, Jr., for all of their differences, provide a threefold warning to contemporary society about the dangers and costs of the fragmented, rootless and often shallow individualism being produced by our educational and social structures.[6]

Christians might, at this point, remember the second part of Jesus' Great Commandment: "Love your neighbor as yourself" (Mt 29:39). All of the preceding arguments from below (including appealing to our self-interest or social needs) might, after all, be caught up in a much more profound command of God. I believe that it is in your neighbor's interest and in society's interest—as well as in your own interest—for *you* to develop a sensitive Christian mind. So too it is an act of love to your neighbors to urge and assist *them* toward this goal.

Christian Minds, Not Intellectualism

In brief, this is the basic case for a Christian mind. Let me stress one more time that I am not advocating *intellectualism* in the Christian life! We must give our brains to God. But we are more than brains. I do indeed want to urge people to develop their minds under the lordship of Jesus Christ. Mindless emotionalism or traditionalism, segmented, fragmented lives and ignorance disguised as simple faith are all terrible deformations of Christian discipleship. But so is arid, dry intellectualism. As you will see in the pages ahead, developing a Christian mind is but one crucial aspect of faithful discipleship.

You will also discover that the primary thrust of this book is directed to individual disciples. I will have plenty to say about the community essential to such individuals. And I will give some attention to the institutions relevant to the subject. But, while I am generally positive about the institutionally focused reforms and dreams of authors like Newman, Holmes, Malik and Illich, my focus is more on the individual's quest for a Christian mind. I have less interest (*less* does not mean *no*!) in remodeling the great institutions of our era than I have in helping disciples to negotiate a fruitful, faithful path through those labyrinths—a path which, I hope, will scatter salt and light wherever it wends its way.

For Ellen, Stan, Bill and Debbie, my four friends introduced earlier, the idea of developing a Christian mind and of relating their faith to their fields of study and work has been an exciting challenge. There is no question that they would like to develop Christian minds. Each of them feels like they are faced with unconquered territory in their study and work. For Ellen and Debbie, being raised in Christian homes and churches laid the foundation for their interest in developing Christian minds. Stan and Bill, on the other hand, became Christians in high school and university, respectively, and the quest to explore the implications of Jesus' lordship is a relatively recent phenomenon. Ellen has strong support from her husband; Stan's roommates and Debbie's mom are suspicious of anything smacking of what they call *intellectual Christianity*. Stan's and Bill's parents are not Christians and are impatient with any excessive zeal for things Christian. Bill's wife is a devoted Christian but has wearied of student poverty and looks forward to his getting a paying job!

In each case, however, the command and invitation of Jesus and Scripture have been decisive for our four friends. They are on their way.

For Reflection or Discussion

1. What, if anything, has been your previous experience with developing a Christian mind? Have you ever tried to relate your Christianity to your field of study or your job? What happened?

2. What might be some of the most important integration points in your studies or work, where the biblical message speaks fairly directly to you and your situation?

3. Can you think of additional biblical texts or practical reasons (not mentioned in this chapter) why developing a Christian mind is important?

4. What costs do you think this endeavor might have for you personally?

Notes

[1]Perpetrators of this prejudice think that talk about a Christian mind is appropriate only after one's devotional or evangelistic practices are in order and one's secular training is more or less complete and coherent. My argument is that biblically and practically such sequencing is terribly misguided.

[2]These are four students I have worked with. I have changed their names and modified some details in their stories to be able to include issues often faced by other students I have known (for example, I invented Stan's parents and roommates in this book because they represent fairly common circumstances for people like him).

[3]Oliver R. Barclay, The Intellect and Beyond (Grand Rapids, Mich.: Zondervan, 1985), p. 10.

[4]See David W. Gill, Peter the Rock: Extraordinary Insights from an Ordinary Man (Downers Grove, Ill.: InterVarsity Press, 1986), for discussion of Peter's Christian thought and experience.

[5]See John Howard Yoder, The Politics of Jesus (Grand Rapids, Mich.: Eerdmans, 1972).

[6]See Robert N. Bellah et al., Habits of the Heart: Individualism and Commitment in American Life (Berkeley, Calif.: University of California, 1985); Allan Bloom, The Closing of the American Mind (New York: Simon and Schuster, 1987); and E. D. Hirsch, Jr., Cultural Literacy: What Every American Needs to Know (Boston, Mass.: Houghton Mifflin, 1987).

THE CHALLENGE OF A TECHNO-PLURALISTIC •WORLD•

2

Having a Christian mind means that in every situation we try to think from the perspective of Jesus Christ, acknowledging him as Lord, Savior and God. It means subordinating and integrating all truth to the Truth, all facts to the Fact, all values to the Value revealed in Jesus Christ. This task has been part of the calling of the people of God from the very beginning. And in every place and time it has been challenged by forces and circumstances which opposed faithfulness to the Lord. There is an inescapable tension between the will of God and the will of a world substantially alienated from its Creator. Yet it is our calling not to flee but to live and think as God's people·within this world.

Whether it is more difficult to form Christian minds in our era than it has been in other times is impossible to say. In any case, the challenge we face in the contemporary world is formidable. The challenge wears a new face in the late twentieth century. Our situation is in certain key respects different from that encountered by our predecessors, and it is to this difference we must turn in this chapter. In discussing our situation I am thinking primarily of the technologically advanced, liberal, democratic West. As more and more of the globe is drawn into the path of Western Civilization, my discussion will have correspondingly broader application. But I do not doubt that developing a Christian mind faces specific and different challenges, for example, in Iran, the Soviet Union, Israel or Zimbabwe.

It is my intention to concentrate on the external, cultural, contextual challenges we face today. However, I would note that we are also challenged *internally* by our proneness to sloth, fear and ignorance. Laziness and weariness, obviously, frustrate the formation of Christian minds. And out of fear we may hold back—what happens if I discover I should change my ways? So we may continue in ignorance of the call and command of God, of the obligation and the adventure to think Christianly.

The formation of a Christian mind is challenged often enough *socially* by neighbors, friends, relatives, fellow-Christians and co-workers who ignore, scorn or actively oppose our attempts to think and live out our faith in a thorough, holistic way. In Stan's case, his parents are non-Christian immigrants from Hong Kong, and his roommates are cynical about any attempt to relate Christian faith to vocational or social issues. And let us not forget that, according to the Word of God, we will be challenged *cosmically* by the principalities and powers in their war against heaven. These internal, social and cosmic challenges are very real and not to be minimized. Part of our response must consist in knowing and communicating the argument for developing a Christian mind. But knowing an argument is not enough to sustain our faithfulness against such challenges. We will also need to cultivate righteous, peaceful, joyful discipleship in close relationship with God and other disciples (Rom 14:17).

Pluralism as Curse and Blessing

My task in this chapter, however, is to examine the essential aspects of the external challenge in the face of which our Christian minds must be shaped. For many Christian analysts, the dominant characteristic of our era is secularism or secular humanism.[1] The great challenge, then, is to articulate and implement Christian values and programs against the great secularist enemy. Some writers rashly speak of a secularist conspiracy, as though a real unity existed among the opponents of Christianity. In my view, secularism is but one element of a multi-faceted opposition.

But I am persuaded that the first word about the challenge we face today is *pluralism,* not secularism. I mean this in a very simple sense: we are confronted by multiplicity, variety, diversity, fragmentation, specialization. Unity, coherence, wholeness? It can't be found—not on the surface at any rate. My Silicon Valley student, Stan, is faced by a sort of traditional cultural Confucianism in his parents, a dualistic Fundamentalism in his roommates, and a fast-lane high-tech existence at his company. We live and think in a pluralistic, as opposed to a monistic (or even dualistic), culture. We are confronted by a bewildering variety of problems, ideas, values, programs and options. Many of these options are in fact religious, even Christian.[2] Thus our challenge is not merely choosing a Christian mind over against a secular one; it is also a problem of sorting among various Christian proposals, figuring out how to relate to many religious as well as secular perspectives.

Pluralism, in the sense just defined, confronts us with a set of difficult problems, to be sure. But I want also to note that it is not without its benefits as a social and cultural context. Quite frankly, I am unimpressed by most examples of monistic societies. We are all at least somewhat familiar with the price of unity and the elimination of pluralism in the Soviet Union or Iran or Nazi Germany. But I must confess that I don't find John Calvin's sixteenth-century Geneva very desirable either. Nor am I attracted to the theory or practice of Abraham Kuyper and his Dutch Reformed colleagues a century ago. Give us the unstable air of pluralism any day rather than the benefits of someone else's decisions about what's good for us.

Overchoice can be a bit overwhelming, but we can prefer it to *underchoice* on the basis of plenty of historical evidence and even personal experience. But let me also point out a much more important reason to welcome pluralism: the Bible calls us to be strangers in (but not of) the world; we are designated salt in the earth, sheep among wolves, and light in the world. A genuine pluralism means we have the cultural space to act as these foreign agents in the world. Our call is not to unify, master and manage the society, but to bear witness to it with truth and love. I think we should, therefore, thank God for the degree of freedom pluralism brings with it—and struggle to preserve such freedom, even if that means standing up to misguided Christians (or non-Christians) trying to ram their agendas down the world's throat.

Still, pluralism creates particular problems and challenges for a Christian mind, and to those I now turn. Pluralism grows in part out of intellectual, political and institutional changes with long histories. Traditional sources of cultural unity and stability (agreement in politics and religion, for example) have been in retreat for centuries. I will not retrace this familiar terrain in the history of the West. Instead, let me begin by suggesting that much of the challenge of pluralism is a product of various forms of *mobility* increasingly characteristic of our society these past two centuries.

Geographic mobility has meant that people move, changing residences, neighbors and environments with increasing frequency and often significant distance. Stan and Debbie still live near or with their parents, but Ellen and Bill are hundreds of miles away from their family roots. But even if you are not among the transient, your neighbors probably are, and you find yourself in the company of many people, with as many perspectives, who have joined your neighborhood, school and workplace. These new neighbors bring new ideas, options, values and histories with them.

If you are among the many who make a geographical move, you are not only moving *to* a new location but *away from* somewhere else. Family, neighborhood and church—the social contexts we lose when leaving—have traditionally been the primary sources of education, support and accountability. If your parents and grandparents are Christian, for example, they nurture, advise and counsel you; they support you emotionally and spiritually as well as materially. There is an accountability that continues to have special force when you are near them (or likely to have your daily life intersect with theirs). There is such a thing as family honor and a shared family (or neighborhood or church) story which carries certain values.

Many people, of course, are understandably happy and relieved to escape the gaze of overzealous parents. But we must face the fact that we are more vulnerable, more fragile, as we are uprooted by our geographic mobility. Deprived of a traditional community of nurture and accountability, values such as fidelity, honesty, generosity, peacefulness and creativity are in increased jeopardy. Many Christians today are relatively isolated and autonomous, cut loose from any significant tradition or community with a long-term commitment to sustain them. This is part of our challenge: we are now on our own more than ever.

Consider next vocational and educational mobility. It was traditional for centuries that children would follow their parents' vocational footsteps. No longer. Most of us enter professions quite different from what our parents did (my dad was an accountant for a large San Francisco corporation). Among our four friends, only Bill is following family tradition in becoming a doctor like his dad. The reason why this is important should be fairly obvious: we spend at least half of the waking time in our life either studying and preparing for work, or carrying it out.

The Christian mind must be developed in our education and work—not just in our personal, church or leisure time. If you are in a different vocation from your parents, however, their own acquired wisdom about thinking Christianly on the job is not directly applicable to your situation. In bygone days a Christian farmer could teach his children Christian ways of work, rest and care for the earth, animals, customers, hired help and so on. Some of this is transferable (in general outline) to the son or daughter practicing law on Wall Street, but not with any specificity.

Mobility means that people encounter new geographic settings and new jobs. We could also discuss the impact of mobility on church experience (people change churches; they abandon denominational tradition; pastors move), friendship (often shallow and of short duration), and school experience (frequency of transfer from one school to another, one major to another—so much for a unified education!). In short, mobility brings freedom but also a substantial challenge to the formation of an integrated Christian mind.

In addition to mobility, the educational-vocational milieu has itself been radically changed by the proliferation of new specializations, increased complexity, and the expanded scope of the work life and its consequences. New jobs are generated endlessly in our era. Old jobs are modified. Consider nursing, which has a long history of traditional values and perspectives. Even if your mother was a nurse and you live with your parents (thus negating the force of my arguments about mobility), your challenge as a modern nurse will be quite different from your mother's. She will still have important things to share about thinking and working Christianly as a nurse, but you will face very new problems of job specialization, new medical procedures, and the modification in the role of the nurse in our time (like being simultaneously an advocate for patients' rights as well as an assistant to the doctor). This will probably be the case for Bill since his father was a general family physician in private practice, and Bill is inclined to join a large clinic and become a specialist.

The same could be said for other jobs (law, business and others): there are vast numbers of new specializations bringing new questions and problems and lacking traditions of humane, ethical or Christian values. Computerization in all fields has brought new challenges. Many new domains have been entered; old domains have been minutely subdivided. *Far from confronting an aggressive secularist tradition of thinking, one is likely to encounter bewildering novelty with no interpretive framework whatsoever.*

It is not merely that the number of job specializations has mushroomed, but their individual complexity has increased, mainly as a result of technology. The morality of human reproduction, to take one example, is vastly complicated by modern technology. So the stakes associated with our work may be significantly heightened today. While our work may be focused more narrowly, its impact on others may be much greater. A traditional carpenter, for example, could change his hours, prices or style of furniture and affect only a few dozen people. The modern particle physicist or city planner or legal specialist might, with a small advance, trigger an impact on thousands or millions of people. Stan's computer work may have this potential; Ellen's banking department activities affect thousands of housing loan applicants. Although our work may rarely, or perhaps never, have this sort of observable consequence, a Christian mind must confront the possible scope and impact of what we do.

Finally, we must note the speed, pressure, distraction and exhaustion of modern existence. We have pluralism and multiplicity on an awesome scale, and it is all experienced as rapid movement. One lives and thinks under tremendous pressure. Developing a unified Christian mind requires time for thought, study, reflection, conversation and prayer—and this is in short supply in our distracted, competitive environment. We can no longer count on nature to bound our existence. Who stops working or running around any more because the sun goes down? Who turns down a task because it is fifty (or five hundred) miles away? Darkness and distance used to bound us and force some evening conversation around the fireplace. No longer! Nor does our culture assist us in finding time and space for reflection. There are very few places where you cannot shop, bank, work or travel twenty-four hours a day, seven days a week.

And so the first level on which the formation of a Christian mind is contested is the sheer quantity of factors pressing upon our shrinking personal space. The call remains valid: "Whatever you do, whether in word or deed, do it all in the name of the Lord Jesus" (Col 3:17). But the "whatever" we are doing is very new, complex and demanding—and we are often alone in a swirling, noisy, anonymous crowd as we do it. The first challenge will be to gain some kind of control of our lives and time, establishing priorities which promise, before too long, to illuminate what "the name of the Lord Jesus" implies for our thought and work.

Technological Infrastructure

In view of this bewildering pluralism, what, we may ask, holds everything together? Are there connecting threads which run through all this diversity? Is there a sort of common infrastructure to our civilization which challenges the formation of a Christian mind? Various studies of civil religion have sought to understand the values treated as sacred in our society, along with the texts, rituals and pedagogy by which these are transmitted.[3] Certainly money and material possessions (consumerism), personal pleasure and fulfillment (narcissism, hedonism), and political power loom large as possible common links in our pluralistic world.

More generally, secularism (or secular humanism) has been proposed, especially by Christians, as the common theme of our culture: the worship of humanity, of the creature instead of the Creator. I do not think that there is evidence to suggest a conscious conspiracy of secular humanists against those who believe God. The rise of New Age religious phenomena, occult and spiritualist movements, even in the intellectual and political centers of our society, ought to caution us that secularism is not unequivocally dominant.[4]

I do not mean to suggest that secularization is a myth, of course.[5] Undeniably there has been an institutional secularization in Western societies over the past two or three centuries. Schools, for example, are now run by the state instead of the organized church. The calendar calls for fewer religious holidays, and the sabbath has been deprived of official religious justification. Churches have been disestablished or separated from public and state institutions. So far as this institutional secularization or laicization goes, I think Christians should welcome it provided that the secular, public arena is open and adequately receptive to the salting and illuminating influence of Christian minds as part of the larger whole, and provided that room is granted for more specific Christian institutions (churches, schools and businesses) to exist.

A second kind of secularization is more subtle. This is not institutional but ideological or intellectual secularization. Ideological secularism is the practice of excluding, ignoring or bracketing out God's truth and reality in the conduct of thought and life. This is to be expected, of course, of nonbelievers. Christians should respond to ideological secularists with evangelism and an invitation to reflect on God's Word from beyond this *saeculum* (the immanent world). (Evangelism in this sense is appropriate not only for secularists but for religious types who listen to other voices from beyond!)

The real problem with ideological secularism is not with some godless congress or faculty, but with intellectually secular (though personally or churchly pious) *Christians!*—Christians who read the Bible and pray at breakfast (good so far!) but then go to class or the office and think and work exactly in the pattern and style of the surrounding world. Secular Christianity, not secular paganism, is the great enemy of the Christian mind and the gospel.

Beneath the pluralistic, chaotic fabric of life (including new religious movements and secular approaches to religion; consumerism; narcissism; hedonism; and politicism) is a powerful technological infrastructure with which a Christian mind must contend. Jacques Ellul calls it *Technique.*[6] Both a spirit and a method, Technique refers to a global, ever-expanding way of thinking and working. The problem of Technique is not with particular technologies, still less with particular machines, electronic or otherwise. Technique is the method of reducing every phenomenon to rational analysis, reducing what is qualitative to quantitative consideration, thinking and working only in relation to measurable results. It is the worship of measurable effectiveness. Technique is raving rationalism. Dominant in scientific methodology and technology, it rules with equal strength in bureaucracy, advertising, marketing, public relations, psychotherapy and other fields.

Question: What do my son's Sikh mathematics teacher, my congressman Ronald Dellums, George Bush's doctor, Jerry Falwell's fund raiser, an Iranian Muslim graduate student in economics, a Transcendental Meditation instructor, and most church-growth strategists have in common? *Answer:* a commitment to thinking and working under the rule of Technique. Despite the surface pluralism represented by a religious Sikh or Muslim, a radical Black politician, a Fundamentalist, a doctor, a missionary and a TM devotee, each of these people (like almost everyone else) works forty or more hours a week obeying the technological logic of seeking the one best way, the method that produces measurable results. Ellen's banking and Bill's medicine are invaded by technology on a grand scale. Stan's work is totally focused on expanding and strengthening technology. Similarly, most of us are trying to find better computer programs and services—more efficient methods for getting more work done.

Make no mistake: technical procedures do produce results, often awesome and wonderful results. The difficulties are twofold: First, technical operations always produce negative effects as well as positive ones which, if detected or cared about, become the justification for further technical operations—and the cycle continues. Mobility as described earlier is one example of this feature of Technique. The second and even greater difficulty is that the ensemble, the spirit of Technique, progressively excludes nonmeasurable, supra-rational, nonproductive—but very important—aspects of human existence. Technology works better without these—and we worship what works.

Even such activities as tennis, meditation, prayer and camping trips are usually justified by the criteria of Technique: they are considered valid because they produce results; they prepare us for more effective work. But the surest test of whether something has the status of being sacred is to put it in question. Whenever I argue that Technique has quasi-divine status, people rise to protest that this is not the case, that Technique is a neutral tool and not the Good today. Invisible, omnipotent, omniscient, omnipresent and not open to criticism: sounds like a god to me.

Our task will be to reverse the process and challenge Technique in the name of spiritual truth and values, tradition, personal relationships and even play. Instead of meekly (or enthusiastically) welcoming the invasion of Technique into the church's planning and activities, the practice of prayer, sexual relationships, parenting, city planning and advertising, we must make a determined, conscious choice to subordinate Technique to a higher truth, an eternal set of values and virtues.

Subordinate does not mean *eliminate*. But instead of ending with a bottom line of profits, feasibility and marketability, we must ask "Is it right and good in relation to the Right and Good we know in Jesus Christ?" When, and only when, Christians commit themselves to this sort of thought process—rooted in Christ's perspective and with Christ's bottom line—will the educational, business, political, economic and social world be truly salted and illuminated.

The means we employ are inextricably bound up with the ends we seek. The means affect the character of the end; they do not play some neutral role and quietly disappear. If we employ technical means, we will have technical ends. A Christian mind cannot, therefore, question only whether products are beneficial and God-honoring, but we must concentrate equally on whether the means to such ends are godly.

For Ellen's banking and Bill's medicine, the questions raised by the technological invasion have to do with the relation of (presumably) efficient techniques for handling masses of customers or patients with the quality of individual, personal care and concern. Can the latter be preserved in banking and health care? For Stan the major questions have to do with potential applications of his technological advances: will his work contribute to human life? to God's purposes?

Fragile Freedom

The issue is not so much *no god* (secularism) as *new god* (Technique). This new god is all the more powerful because it is judged to be neutral and therefore beyond question. Technique rules and we lay down our lives in worship. This is why humanism is hardly the appropriate description of modern life. God has not been replaced by the Human but by Technique, to which human life is subordinated. Our lives are crushed and directed by the quest for quantifiable growth, measurable success and rational efficiency (the Technical Trinity). This god promises everything (today or tomorrow!) to the all-important Self as well as (for those interested) to all nations and social groups.

Should we be awakened to contest this rule, we discover not just one tyrant to battle, but a bewildering variety of problems and options, technical, educational, geographic, religious, political and so on. And where is there an in-depth, critical, holistic perspective within which to situate a coherent, liveable response to all this? We find ourselves alone, separated from tradition, family, deep friendships and vital community. We face complex new specializations which appear to defy incorporation within a unified, healthy Christian mind.

We are faced with an awesome freedom. We may move, change jobs and churches, organize and reorganize our lives, read whatever we wish, dress and live as we choose, spend our leisure as we desire. And we can thank God for this freedom, unstable as it may leave our lives. But such freedom is fragile and may conceal a deeper servitude to Technique and its hosts. True freedom must be received as a gift from the Lord of space and time and then lived out in full consciousness before the Giver of the gift. Otherwise we may think we are free from slavery in Egypt only to discover we have been blindly enslaved to new taskmasters in the wilderness.

A heavy, depressing burden? Not necessarily. Our situation can be the stage for an exhilarating lifelong adventure. The technical mentality insists on immediate, observable results. The God of the Bible is patient, caring and willing to take the whole of our life span to build character, quality and meaning into our experience. There will be failures and mistakes, as well as victories and rewards. The challenge of the Christian mind in our techno-pluralistic world is not to change the whole world this week or year, but to take the first step, then the next . . .

For Reflection or Discussion

1. What is similar—and different—between your life and work and that of your parents? (geographic location, education, vocation, church). How, if at all, have your roots assisted you in coping with pluralism?

2. In what ways—if at all—has Technique ruled around you in your educational, work, church or personal environment? Is Technique a better one-word description for our era than Secularism, and if so, how?

3. What are some of the things the Bible says are wrong or defective about our world? How are these described by techno-pluralism?

4. What is the biggest challenge you face in living with the effects of a techno-pluralistic society?

Notes

[1]This is argued intelligently by Harry Blamires in his modern classic *The Christian Mind* (London: SPCK, 1963; Ann Arbor, Mich.: Servant Books, 1978). It is argued unintelligently by dozens of popular American Christian authors.

[2]Consider the political proposals of Christians such as Jim Wallis and *Sojourners* magazine, Jerry Falwell and the New Christian Right, R. J. Rushdoony and the various factions of Christian Reconstructionists, and (my preference) Vernard Eller's *Christian Anarchy: Jesus' Primacy Over the Powers* (Grand Rapids, Mich.: Eerdmans, 1987).

[3]See Robert N. Bellah, "Civil Religion in America," in *Religion in America*, ed. W. G. McLoughlin and R. Bellah (Boston, Mass.: Houghton Mifflin, 1968), pp. 3-23.

[4]See Jacques Ellul, *The New Demons* (New York: Seabury, 1975).

[5]David W. Gill, "Secularism," *Evangelical Dictionary of Theology*, ed. Walter A. Elwell (Grand Rapids, Mich.: Baker, 1984), pp. 996-97.

[6]I use a capital T to indicate that we are dealing with a large-scale, collective reality, not individual techniques for reading fast, brewing beer or driving on icy roads. *Technique* is a better term than *technology* because the latter has such strong associations with engineering and applied science. See Jacques Ellul, *The Technological Society* (New York: Vintage, 1964). The original French title, translated, is: Technique: the stake [challenge, issue] of the century. See also Jacques Ellul, *Presence of the Kingdom* (New York: Seabury, 1970); David W. Gill, *The Word of God in the Ethics of Jacques Ellul*, ATLA Monograph No. 20, (Metuchen, N. J.: Scarecrow Press, 1984); and Stephen V. Monsma, ed., *Responsible Technology* (Grand Rapids, Mich.: Eerdmans, 1986).

THE STRENGTH
AND WEAKNESS
OF TODAY'S
•UNIVERSITY•
3

The problem of developing a Christian mind is closely related to university education because so many of us spend so many years of our lives submitting to intellectual formation in such places. Factually and technically, today's universities offer extraordinary possibilities for knowledge and specialized expertise. The university-trained parts of our minds can become extremely muscular and potent. For several reasons, however, such intellectual muscle has little in common with wisdom, moral depth, or spiritual sensitivity and understanding. In one sense today's universities pose a threat to society by arming graduates with powerful tools—but without the holistic wisdom and character necessary to employ these powers in the best interests of themselves, their neighbors or God. It is the intellectual equivalent of selling guns to people without worrying about their psychological stability!

Today's university both reflects and affects the techno-pluralistic world discussed in the previous chapter. Analysts like Charles Habib Malik, for example, stress the direct and indirect influence of the university on contemporary life.[1] The movers and shakers in our world are trained in the university. The ideas and discoveries of the university have sometimes dramatic impact on the world of business, politics and the arts. The university has developed and extended the sway of technique and the specialization that contributes to pluralism. Its analyses have undermined traditional authorities and practices found to be irrational and eccentric.

But one can argue the other way as well. Consider the influence of government funding on the directions of scientific and technological research in the university. No money, no research. And when the business world cries out for computer experts or MBA's or the litigious society invites hoards of new attorneys, that's what the university provides. In today's democratized environment where everyone who can spell their name is assumed to have a right to higher education, public and political pressure forces universities to open up and adapt. Nor should anyone assume that the university is operated by disinterested intellectuals living off honoraria! Whatever else it remains, the university is a big business appealing to the student market (and to taxpayers) for survival, salaries and legitimacy. As Clark Kerr, former president of the University of California, has written, it is a "great cliché about the university" to picture it "as autonomous, a cloister, when the historical fact is that it has always responded, but seldom so quickly as today, to the desires and demands of external groups."[2]

A Christian mind needs to be developed by undergraduates as well as graduates, by those preparing for vocations and careers as well as those out in the marketplace. Both for those currently in the university and those who have been there in the past, this chapter continues our quest to form Christian minds by examining the strength and weakness of the university. My approach will take the form of a brief historical look at the university as an institution, followed by a review of some important critiques of its status and operations. A summary of its strengths and weaknesses will conclude this chapter.

From University to Multiversity

The university's long history formally begins in the twelfth century with the founding of the universities of Salerno, Bologna and Paris, followed soon after by Oxford, Cambridge and dozens of others throughout Europe. The first universities were religiously centered communities of scholarship, learning and professional formation (medicine, law, theology and education). These were not merely centers for acquiring professional skills, but included education in the liberal arts with classic literature, mathematics, science, philosophy, grammar, rhetoric, and then-queen of the sciences—theology. The university (from the Latin *universitas,* meaning *the whole)* intended to prepare the intellectual, spiritual and moral leaders of society by giving them broad, deep, wise, morally sensitive, unified minds. In the seventeenth century, Harvard, William and Mary, and Yale—the first three American universities— carried on the same tradition and ideals.

During the eighteenth century, new universities at Princeton, Columbia, and especially Pennsylvania added pragmatic studies in geography, applied science, navigation and other fields to this liberal arts core. Specialized professional schools of law, medicine and theology were set up within the structure of the university as an approvement on traditional apprenticeships. In the nineteenth century, Johns Hopkins University was the first American university to follow the newer German graduate research model featuring the seminar system. In the same era federal land grant universities, the rise of the elective system, academic majors and a general democratization of higher educational opportunities all contributed to the end of the traditional notion of the university as a religiously centered exercise in intellectual wholeness.

Still, even through the end of the nineteenth century, most American universities continued to pursue a holistic, integrated, morally sensitive set of objectives. This not only affected individual classes and lectures but was reflected in a common requirement for all senior students to take a course (often called "moral philosophy"), usually taught by the college president, which drew together the undergraduate body of learning and honed the ethical sensitivities of the students about to enter the marketplace.[3]

As the twentieth century unfolded, this senior requirement was dropped almost everywhere. With the rise of the elective system and the rapid growth of specialization, a common core-curriculum became impossible. But along with the demands of specialization in a diversified curriculum, the growing influence of the methods and epistemology of the natural sciences also undermined the traditional ideals. The cult of scientific objectivity, suggesting ethical and spiritual detachment, affected the humanities as well as the rising new social sciences. Gains in specialized technical knowledge were accompanied by losses in reformist zeal. (The academic must be refined and objective, after all.) Moral values retreated before value freedom, and neutral, descriptive objectivity. Sociology, for example, began as a passionate, reformist field, but by the 1920s it yielded to passive scientific objectivity.

By 1964 only twenty-seven of one hundred universities surveyed required so much as one philosophy course of their graduates, to say nothing of religion or theology![4] Of course, even the philosophy and religion departments by this time had to suppress normative, prescriptive interests in favor of scientific, descriptive, academically respectable neutrality, or else give up their standing in the modern university. The university had abandoned its quest to provide unified, much less Christian or ethical, minds.

Traditionally, the undergraduate university curriculum provided an education in the liberal arts with generous doses of history, literature and language. Then in graduate schools of law, medicine, business or other fields, or on the job itself, students would be trained in a particular vocation. Even if the grand dream of a unified education was in eclipse, professionals would still be integrated into the moral ethos of their particular calling. Today's professional schools have become little more than technical training centers. Only in the post-Watergate era have professional ethics courses reappeared in some of these schools. Undergraduate education (despite recent noises to the contrary) has become a smorgasbord of electives primarily valuable for amusement or job-skill acquisition. Allan Bloom's sarcasm is undisguised: "So the student must navigate among a collection of carnival barkers, each trying to lure him into a particular sideshow." The student who looks for holistic personal formation is an "embarrassment to most universities" for "he is the one to whom they have nothing to say."[5] For many of its enrollees, the university is a job-skill training center, or a place to hide out before entering the pressure cooker of the working world.

Lest all of the preceding sound too cynical, I would say that somewhere on that smorgasbord there is almost everything necessary to construct a fairly broad and deep education. But the university does not require such broad, unified learning for its certification, nor are these gigantic institutions very good at assisting students in choosing such a program. Like the world itself, the university offers powerful technical skills, specialized knowledge and a myriad of possibilities. The burden, however, falls on the lonely individual to construct an education or a life out of these possibilities.

Spouting, fuming and blaming the modern university will accomplish nothing, of course. Spelling out some utopian, idealistic vision for major reform of today's university is a dubious activity. Building alternative Christian universities of similar scale strikes me as equally utopian. Acquiescently passing through today's "multiversity" and moving into the marketplace with doctoral skills and a kindergarten world view is common, but for reasons noted earlier, unacceptable. So what can we do?

Critics and Reformers

Although it is now more than a century since its initial publication, John Henry Cardinal Newman's classic study *The Idea of a University* remains an important benchmark for our evaluation of the university.[6] Newman's immediate project was the founding of the new Catholic University of Ireland (which he served as first president from 1851-58). The project itself was not a great success for several reasons including money, phil-

osophical conflicts and Irish-English relations, but it yielded one of the
great educational treatises of all time.

Newman's central concerns were to ensure that theology was included in a university education (otherwise the university's claim to
pursue universal knowledge was betrayed), and that the liberal arts,
rather than the "useful arts and sciences," should remain its "direct and
principal concern." Theology has the largest field of vision of any
science and Newman recognized that we "will soon break up into frag-
ments the whole circle of secular knowledge if [we] begin with the
mutilation of the divine." Newman believed "that all knowledge forms
one whole . . . intimately knit together" and that the true university
should promote such unified learning.[7]

"In a word, religious truth is not only a portion but a condition of
general knowledge. To blot it out is nothing short . . . of unravelling the
web of university teaching." A "refusal to recognize theological truth in
a course of universal knowledge . . . is not only the loss of theology, it
is the perversion of other sciences."[8] This is so because without theology, other sciences and fields will attempt to provide their own answers
to fill the void.

With regard to the aims of university education "it is more correct
. . . to speak of a university as a place of education, than of instruction
. . . Education is a higher word; it implies an action upon our mental
nature, and the formation of a character; it is something individual and
permanent, and is commonly spoken of in connexion with religion and
virtue." Instruction may impart specific skills and knowledge but true
education forms a great intellect, "one which takes a connected view
of old and new, past and present, far and near, and which has an
insight into the influence of all these on one another; without which
there is no whole, and no centre. That only is true enlargement of mind
which is the power of viewing many things at once as one whole, of
referring them severally to their true place in the universal system, of
understanding their respective values, and determining their mutual
dependence." This "general culture of mind" is a worthy object in its
own right but it is also "the best aid to professional and scientific study"

and "best enables [one] to discharge his duties to society."[9]

We don't need to share Newman's enthusiastic Roman Catholicism or all of his detailed prescriptions to see that his basic vision for the university would have gone some distance toward the preparation of unified Christian minds. But a century after Newman, this vision is dead in the water: theology is in total disarray and retreat in today's universities, job skills predominate over the liberal arts as educational objectives, and the only unity in one's education is the hidden dominance of Technique.

In contrast to Newman's vision, Clark Kerr, former president of the University of California, proposed "The Idea of a Multiversity" in 1963. "The university started as a single community—a community of masters and students. It may even be said to have had a soul in the sense of a central animating principle. Today the large American university is, rather, a whole series of communities and activities held together by a common name, a common governing board, and related purposes."[10] Whether we like it or not, this "multiversity" is a fact that we must understand and come to terms with, according to Kerr.

The multiversity is composed of many internal communities with as many purposes. It "stands for a certain standard of performance, a certain degree of respect, a certain historical legacy, a characteristic quality of spirit." It reflects the pluralism of society and is subject to the demands of many interest groups from without and within. It is partly the result of the historical circumstances noted earlier (the rise of the German research model, the elective system and others) and partly the mirror image of society. The multiversity supplies society with knowledge; it increasingly acts as a cultural center for communities; it sometimes fulfills the promise of being a true city of intellect where it "can have great potential roles to play in the reconciliation of the war between the future and the past, and the solution—one way or another—of the war between the ideological giants who now rend the world with their struggles."[11]

Arthur Holmes, a philosophy professor at the greatest of the American evangelical colleges, Wheaton, correctly notes that the modern secular university "compartmentalizes religion and treats it as peripheral or even irrelevant to large areas of life and thought." The formerly unifying religious perspective has disintegrated and "education today is rootless, or at best governed by pragmatism and the heterogeneity of viewpoints that makes ours both a secular and a pluralistic society. The result is a *multi*versity not a *uni*versity, an institution without a unifying world-view and so without unifying educational goals." Christian professors and students in secular universities are reduced to witnessing, and "the primary impact is . . . a *conjunction* of Christian witness with secular education rather than an integration of faith and learning into an ed-ucation that is itself Christian."[12]

Holmes proposes the Christian college as the heir to the Christianly integrative educational aims of Newman. Holmes is, I think, correct that not much integration of faith and learning has been occurring among Christians on secular campuses. But my own visits to Christian college campuses have not turned up much integration there either. Ellen, a graduate of a Christian college often compared with Wheaton, found no significant attempts at creative Christian perspective on anything except religious studies!

If everyone thought as Professor Holmes, the Christian college might be a major source of a revival of Christian minds in our era.[13] In any event, the vast majority of Christians (like Bill, Stan and Debbie) will continue to attend multiversities. And therein lies our challenge to counter this *conjunction* with true *integration.*

A contemporary review is the dramatic, blistering essay by former United Nations leader Charles Habib Malik, *A Christian Critique of the University* (1982). For Malik, "the great universities of the Western world raise fundamental questions from the Christian point of view. They are pretty thoroughly secularized. The prevailing atmosphere in them is not congenial to Christian spiritual values. One wonders if Christ would find himself at home in them, and to a Christian nothing is more serious than if Christ is not at home in the great citadels of learning. . . . The universities, then, directly or indirectly, dominate the world; their influence is so pervasive and total that whatever problem afflicts them is bound to have far-reaching repercussions throughout the entire fabric of Western civilization." Both the secular universities and typical Christian colleges fail to demonstrate "that Jesus Christ has any relevance to the matter and spirit of their scientific research and learning."[14]

Malik develops a ten-point critique of the sciences, including an attack on its arrogance, reductionism, runaway proliferation of knowledge, lack of integration with other fields, myopia, illicit transfer of authority, pride of knowledge and power, evolutionism, monism and atheism. Malik then trains his guns on the humanities with a twenty-one point critique of its naturalism, subjectivism, rationalism, skepticism, analysis (at the price of synthesis), idealism, materialism, technologism, futurism, cynicism, nihilism, Freudianism, relativism, voluntarism, change (denial of any fixity), hurried pace, humanism, monism, immanentism, secularism and atheism. He concludes his critique by urging Christians to attempt to recapture the universities as much as possible by means of brilliant, faithful scholarship. He is dubious about starting over with new universities. His final suggestion is the formation of an institute to "monitor the university for Jesus Christ." Malik's critical comments on the sciences and humanities are, I think, on target. His suggested responses have merit but reflect an over-dependence on a top-down view of change that is not likely to have much impact on the daily lives of Christians being educated in today's universities.

Many other critics, of course, have addressed the state of today's university education. Racism, sexism, militarism and other problems have needed to be faced in the university as well as in the broader society and culture. Ivan Illich's many works raise broad questions of freedom and dependence in relation to educational (and other) institutions. Is a university education liberating its graduates—or training them for further consumption and institutional dependence?[15] Christopher Lasch decries the "decline of critical thought and the erosion of intellectual standards" accompanying our "culture of narcissism."[16] Universities today are failing to provide any sort of broad, unified cultural tradition within which to integrate specialized knowledge and skills.

In a similar vein, E. F. Schumacher criticized the separation of scientific, technical know-how from metaphysical wisdom. By itself, know-how can be dangerous. The basic purpose of education must be the transmission of values, the production of wisdom and the creation of an orderly system of ideas by which to live and to interpret the world. "What is at fault is not specialization, but the lack of depth with which subjects are usually presented, and the absence of metaphysical awareness."[17]

One of the most recent and important discussions of contemporary American culture (and its educational institutions) is *Habits of the Heart* by University of California sociologist Robert Bellah and four colleagues. Reminding us that "the American college through much of the nineteenth century was organized on the assumption that 'higher learning constituted a single unified culture,' " Bellah suggests that "one of the major costs of the rise of the research university and its accompanying professionalism and specialization was the impoverishment of the public sphere." But, Bellah argues, "specialization requires integration; they are not mutually exclusive. . . . [We] have never before faced a situation that called our deepest assumptions so radically into question. Our problems today are not just political. They are moral and have to do with the meaning of life."[18]

Allan Bloom's feisty diatribe against the modern university, *The Closing of the American Mind*, became the surprise sales-leader of nonfiction American books during most of 1987. It was a surprise because the American public's taste for four-hundred-page volumes heavy with German intellectual history has not been evident in the past! Bloom criticizes the modern university for its wimpy capitulation to various social pressures from feminists, Black power groups, 1960s radicals and others. He argues that the classical, nonutilitarian search for truth has everywhere been compromised by a quest for relevance, that the natural sciences, social sciences, humanities and professional schools are desperately weakened by their isolation from each other. Bloom has said much of great value to those who wish to understand contemporary higher education. But, he concludes, "it is difficult to imagine that there is either the wherewithal or the energy within the university to constitute or reconstitute the idea of an educated human being and establish a liberal education again. . . . The matter is still present in the university; it is the form that has vanished. One cannot and should not hope for a general reform. The hope is that the embers do not die out."[19]

Strength and Weakness

As both its defenders and critics agree, today's university is significantly different than it used to be, far from the hopes and dreams of John Henry Newman. Most universities, private or public, religiously affiliated or not, have become too big, too pluralistic, too fragmented and specialized, and too responsive to society's demand for trained technicians to be able to provide graduates with a unified, deep, integrated world view, or a highly motivated moral sensitivity and zeal. Christians who, in joyful obedience to their Lord, pursue the formation of Christian minds will have to look outside the university faculty for assistance.

We must not, however, fail to note the positive side of today's multiversity. Far from damning or abandoning the university, Christians can appreciate its many strengths. First, universities do offer marvelous opportunities for the acquisition of skills, training and knowledge. Who can look over a catalog from a major university without salivating over its course offerings? The sort of knowledge today's universities provide is *essential* in forming a Christian mind, even though it is not *sufficient*. Second, today as never before, the pluralism of the university has expanded to include women as well as men, all races, classes and ages, and endless numbers of foreign students and scholars. I have zero interest in returning to the older model of a male, upper-class, socially homogeneous university. But one has the distinct impression that Bloom would be quite content with that sort of exclusivism.

Third, the diversity and chaos (as well as opportunity) of today's university with its technical obsessions closely mirror the workplace and marketplace. Sooner or later, we will have to cope with this situation. There is a lot more to be said for hammering out a Christian mind and lifestyle in such an environment than for cloistering oneself for four or five years in some unreal, holy enclave. Fourth, the absence of a unified world view and ethical framework in today's university is, in my opinion, much to be preferred over the presence of some second-rate ideology. Better far to study in our chaotic universities than be submitted to a steady diet of state socialist orthodoxy (or Newman's Anglo-Irish Catholicism? or Kuyperian Orthodoxy? or Bloom's philosophy?) which steamrollers all deviants!

I have always loved John Milton's *Areopagitica* speech: "Who can praise a cloistered virtue? Let truth and falsehood grapple! What hath truth to fear in a free and open encounter?" Christians are followers of the Truth, Jesus Christ. But we do not *a priori* possess all truth! Often enough we are ignorant and wrong; non-Christians, likewise, are characterized by both truth and error in their thinking. With humble confidence in Jesus Christ, Christians can develop Christian minds attending to the critical suggestions not only of their brothers and sisters but all of God's creatures. If we cannot learn how to both think and speak our (Christian) mind in the pluralistic university, it will not be any easier for us in the working world after graduation.

And, finally, what about the university itself? By all means let us have Christian scholars and administrators who get involved. But if anything is to be, in Malik's term, *recaptured*, it would more modestly be some adequate space in the forum. I recall some advice to salt the earth and light the world—not to recapture or rule it. What the university can do today, perhaps better than any other institution, is serve as the sponsor and referee for dialog and mutual understanding in our pluralistic society. The university can invite virtually all comers (religious, political, economic, intellectual) to articulate their perspectives and submit to conversation, analysis and criticism in a non-hostile context of freedom.

In sponsoring and refereeing such dialog, society's pluralism will more likely be cooperative than predatory, and the dominant spirit of Technique will be checked and held accountable in a healthy way (by virtue of having to answer to individuals and groups still maintaining various spiritual or cultural values). What has happened in our era is a great takeover of public dialog and conflict by the political and legal institutions. But going to court and going to the polls, litigating and politicizing our conflicts and disagreements inevitably depersonalizes, simplifies, abstracts and hardens our situation. The university can provide the best possible forum for dialog and analysis of our diversity.[20] It is in this way that the university can recover its historic role as moral resource for society.

Concretely and programmatically, this all means that the university should encourage (as it sometimes does) the growth of various independent institutes and centers (Catholic, Protestant, Buddhist, Islamic, Marxist, Feminist, Luddite) on the edges of the campus. The campus must be open to free speech, discussion and advocacy by student and faculty-sponsored political, religious and other groups, provided only that such advocacy is neither coercive or unavoidably disruptive to those uninterested.

It is interesting to note that the University of California has historically been ringed by just such centers. In 1888-90, U. C. president Horace Davis "attempted to surround the University with informal religious centers of all denominations. Some of them would provide housing as part of their physical accommodations. All of them would exert a continuous religious influence that the University, by law, could not itself provide."[21] Today the University of California is in fact ringed by various religious centers: a dozen theological seminaries, at least one Christian fraternity and sorority, headquarters for various campus ministries, and a twelve-year-old graduate school of Christian studies for the laity whose purpose is to assist university graduates in taking the best the university has to offer and then integrating this in a robustly biblical Christian mind.[22] Today's university is under considerable fire. But there is plenty of evidence that, far from being a desperate situation, ours is the hour of unparalleled adventure and possibility!

For Reflection or Discussion
1. How does your university experience compare with the critique of the modern university given in this chapter?

2. What resources (people, programs), if any, are (or were) available during your university days to help you develop an integrated world view or an ethically sensitive perspective on your field?

3. Do you agree with the vision of an expanded public-forum role for today's university? Will it work? Is it likely?

Notes

[1]Charles Habib Malik, *A Christian Critique of the University* (Downers Grove, Ill.:InterVarsity Press, 1982).

[2]Clark Kerr, *The Uses of the University*, 3rd ed. (Cambridge, Mass.: Harvard University Press, 1982), p. 94. What Kerr acknowledges and accepts, Allan Bloom rages against in his best seller, *The Closing of the American Mind* (New York: Simon and Schuster, 1987).

[3]See the fascinating study by Douglas Sloan, "The Teaching of Ethics in the American Undergraduate Curriculum, 1876-1976," in *Ethics Teaching in Higher Education*, Daniel Callahan and Sissela Boks, ed., (Hastings-on-Hudson, N.Y.: The Hastings Center, 1980), pp. 1-57.

[4]Ibid., p. 41.

[5]Bloom, *American Mind*, p. 339.

[6]John Henry Cardinal Newman, *The Idea of a University*, (rev. ed. 1873; reprint ed., New York: Doubleday Image, 1959).

[7]Quotations from ibid., pp. 61, 67, 87.

[8]Ibid., pp. 103, 109.

[9]Ibid., pp. 139, 156, 158, 181, 191.

[10]Kerr, *The Uses of the University*, p. 1.

[11]Kerr, Ibid., pp. 19, 126.

[12]Arthur F. Holmes, *The Idea of a Christian College* (Grand Rapids, Mich.: Eerdmans, 1975), pp. 19, 17.

[13]See, for example, Arthur Holmes, *Contours of a World View* (Grand Rapids, Mich.: Eerdmans, 1983), and Arthur Holmes, ed., *The Making of a Christian Mind* (Downers Grove, Ill.: InterVarsity Press, 1985).

[14]Malik, pp. 13-14, 20, 29.

[15]See Ivan Illich, *Celebration of Awareness: A Call for Institutional Revolution* (New York: Doubleday Anchor, 1970); *Deschooling Society* (New York: Harper & Row, 1970); *Tools for Conviviality* (New York: Harper & Row, 1973); and *Toward a History of Needs* (New York: Pantheon Books, 1977).

[16]Christopher Lasch, *The Culture of Narcissism* (New York: Norton, 1978).

[17]E. F. Schumacher, *Small Is Beautiful: Economics as if People Mattered* (New York: Harper & Row, 1976), p. 95.

[18]Robert N. Bellah et al., *Habits of the Heart: Individualism and Commitment in American Life* (Berkeley, Calif.: University of California Press, 1985), pp. 295,

298-99, 300.

[19]Bloom, *American Mind,* p. 380.

[20]Part of this function is described by James M. Gustafson, "The University as a Community of Moral Discourse," *Journal of Religion,* 53 (1973): 397-409.

[21]Cited in Verne A. Stadtman, *The University of California, 1868-1968* (New York: McGraw-Hill, 1970), p. 100.

[22]I refer to New College Berkeley, where I teach.

SIX MARKS
OF A
CHRISTIAN
•MIND•
4

Have you ever watched people play a game they don't really know how to play? They might be naturally very athletic. They might have a lot of fun. But as you observe, you can't help but wish they knew the real thing. When living in France a few years ago, I happened to see a group of guys out in a field hitting a ball with a stick, then running to some rudimentary base, being chased and roughly tagged out (I guess). With Sherlock Holmesian deductive powers, I figured out before long that they must be playing a primitive form of baseball. Baseball is unknown in France (try to find out even the World Series results in any French newspaper!), so maybe one of these guys had seen a baseball game in Italy or America and had brought back the idea for this game.

Now I'm not criticizing their game or fun. It was fine fun (with the possible exception of the bone-crushing collisions! Had they mixed up

American football and baseball?). But I couldn't help wondering if they would ever get to know (and play) *real* baseball. Would they ever discover the meaning of four balls or three strikes, pitching from a stretch, checking the runners, flashing a sign, the hit-and-run, the curve ball, the suicide squeeze, the grand slam? Would they ever know about Ty Cobb, or the 1919 Black Sox scandal, or Willie Mays?

Their experience was fine . . . but it was like someone eating hamburgers and never discovering prime rib. Like knowing your city park and never seeing Yosemite. Like living in Los Angeles and never seeing San Francisco or Paris. Like watching the Cal Bears play football and never seeing UCLA or USC. Now, all kidding aside, this is the way we should think of the vistas opened up by the development of a Christian mind. Equation: a true baseball mind is to that primitive stick ball mind I saw in France as a truly Christian mind is to the simplistic, confused techno-pluralist mind dominating the world today.

Nurturing and shaping a Christian mind, trusting and loving God with all our mind, means the possibility of seeing life and work in depth. It means a lifelong adventure in meaning, direction, purpose and understanding. It means being absorbed into the vantage point of the Creator, Center and Redeemer of everything. If we do not intentionally cultivate such a Christian mind, we will inexorably be shaped by the university and marketplace into having a consumer mind, technological mind, Wall Street mind or some kindred type. All of these, while having their value, are like being limited to stick ball when we could be playing and loving real American baseball.

So how might we characterize or describe the basic shape and movement of a Christian mind? Harry Blamires's well-known book *The Christian Mind* (1963) discusses six characteristics which define a Christian way of thinking over against the prevailing secular approach. Blamires's six marks of the Christian mind are: supernatural orientation, awareness of evil, conception of truth, acceptance of authority, concern for the person and sacramental cast. Arthur Holmes's *Contours of a World View* (1983) discusses God, persons, truth, values, society and history as constituent dimensions of a Christian world view. Many other authors have discussed the shape of a Christian mind today but, in my view, Blamires's classic discussion is deservedly the point of departure for thinking about the subject—and Holmes's marvelous book is the advanced course (after you finish *The Opening of the Christian Mind*, of course!).[1]

Nevertheless, based on my own study of Scripture (as well as Newman, Holmes, Blamires and others) *and* based on my own experience as student and professor, I want to propose a slightly different account of the marks of a Christian mind, though it has obvious overlap with these other works at various points. These six characteristics describe the *expansion* and the *focusing* of a Christian mind. I submit that they apply to every Christian in every field of study or work. Consciously cultivate these six marks and you will be well on the way to having a Christian mind. We will explore *how* to develop a mind with these characteristics, but we must begin with the *what*, the general contours, the six characteristics of a Christian mind.

A Theological Mind

The first and crucial characteristic of a Christian mind is its expanded field of vision, and then its focus on God within that field. "The fear of the LORD is the beginning of wisdom, and knowledge of the Holy One is understanding" (Prov 9:10). Despite the (sometimes deserved) criticism of Christians as being narrow-minded, the first characteristic of a Christian mind is precisely its openness. A Christian mind must be supremely open and broad, oriented not only to the range of natural, material, empirical and immanent factors, but to the supernatural, supra-temporal, eternal and invisible possibilities. This does not mean being otherworldly (as opposed to this-worldly) but rather both-worldly. It does not imply gullibility or naiveté but simple openness.

Jesus demonstrated this characteristic perfectly. He lived on this earth and showed deep and genuine concern for people, nature, human institutions, hunger, peace, justice—the whole range of this-worldly life. But Jesus also lived and thought in openness to angelic and demonic forces and, above all, the living reality of God the Heavenly Father.

Healing and disease were understood by him not only in this-worldly terms but in relation to a spiritual battle. Jesus lived a life of prayer to God the Father as well as conversation with those around him.

Theology can be defined as God-talk (logos about theos). A theological mind, in my rudimentary definition of the term, is a mind that brings God-talk into conversation. This is not easy today, despite our pluralism, because the worlds of education, business, science and technology are methodologically atheist. Even if individuals are not personally or philosophically atheists, God is bracketed out of most seminars, corporate planning and marketing discussions, court proceedings, surgical operations and so on. When this is treated as a comprehensive picture of truth and reality, we are then in the presence of a narrow-minded materialism, a reductionism. It is what I call ontological myopia, tunnel vision, closed-mindedness.

A theological mind does not necessarily introduce óvert God-talk into every conversation or meeting! To do so may trivialize the whole process, including God. There is much to be gained, for example, by researching and writing a paper exploring ways a materialistic Marxist sociology would analyze a given urban problem. So, too, a Christian attorney might plow through endless cases to discover how a given situation has been adjudicated simply within the bounds of state law. What is sub-Christian is to regard these perspectives as decisive, or as the only relevant analyses. It turns out that God also cares about urban problems and legal justice. There may be principalities and powers at work in the structures of the city and law. A Christian mind must not necessarily quote Scripture at every moment; but before leaving the problem at hand it must take captive and subordinate scientific, technical, legal or other perspectives to the theological perspective. This requires a mind that can grasp many viewpoints and that has taken the time to explore them.

But beware—an open mind is not the same as an empty mind! Allan Bloom has recently pointed out that "there are two kinds of openness, the openness of indifference . . . and the openness that invites us to the quest for knowledge and certitude."[2] Christian minds are not only open to God and the supernatural, they are focused on God as the most important, central and authoritative factor. What God thinks and says about law, justice, money, health, disease, history, race, sex, politics, anxiety or any other subject is more fundamental and important in the end than anything our scientific, rational or technical methods might dictate. God not only illuminates (and adds to) our stockpile of facts—he illuminates values, meaning and the context in which these facts have significance.

Thus, a Christian urban sociologist must carry out excellent, thorough, social-science research not unlike that of his or her colleagues. But in the end this must be enclosed within, ruled by, and perhaps reinterpreted by, the revelation of God with respect to the origin, history, future and meaning of human cities (need we remind ourselves of all that the Bible has to say about cities?). The latter perspective gives a richness and depth to our understanding of, and proposals for, our urban challenge that is much more powerful than the sterile, dry, statistical models of a purely scientific work.

The same sort of illustration could be developed for Christians in the financial world, law, politics, the arts or any other field. For Ellen, as a bank executive, a theological mind means hearing what Jesus and Scripture have to say about money, property, wealth and the practice of charging interest, as well as leadership and management issues. For Bill it means exploring the biblical material on health, illness, death, suffering and healing. For Stan (the computer expert) a theological mind will mean that he locates his development of electronic tools in a robust biblical view of work, stewardship and the relation of values and persons to efficient management of data and work.[3] Stan will need to assess the possible application of his work (to the military, medical, financial and legal worlds). For Debbie, Jesus and Scripture will affect the way she views teaching, the values she employs in literary criticism, and the way she makes choices about career possibilities and priorities.

Most precisely and directly, a theological mind is oriented to Jesus Christ as God's incarnate Word, the fullest, clearest, most accessible expression of God's truth and reality we have available (Heb 1:3; Col

1:15-20). "In [Christ] are hidden all the treasures of wisdom and knowledge [understanding]" (Col 2:3). Penetrating that hidden rootage of wisdom in Jesus is not always simple. But it *is* always an adventure. A Christian mind means going beyond the narrow field of vision in the world around us, crossing old boundaries, exploring new possibilities. This is necessary—and possible—because we are attuned to the God we know in Jesus Christ who himself exceeds all natural bounds and is the author of the new and unforeseen.

An open, Jesus-centered, theological mind: the first and primary mark of a Christian mind.

A Historical Mind

A theological mind is, we might say, *spatially* enlarged and enriched. The second expansion is a *temporal* one: we are required to cultivate an historical mind. Consider St. Paul's statement to the early church at Corinth: "These things [in Israel's history] happened to them as examples and were written down as warnings for us, on whom the fulfillment of the ages has come" (1 Cor 10:11). This brief biblical text illustrates the importance for Christians of being informed by the past, responsibly alive in the present and thoughtful about the future. Oscar Cullmann's *Christ and Time* and many other studies have shown how significant is the Hebrew-Christian view of linear time.[4] God created, preserves, and comes into human history, and he gives it direction from creation to future kingdom. Reality is thus not mere cyclical repetition, nor is it a transcendent "beyond" which minimizes our historical experience. Each point in time is decisive and unique; the totality of history is the texture on which the present occurs.

Jesus, our model, lived fully in the present but drew on the past (near and distant events and writings) in ways both respectful and creative. He warned and promised about the future (near and distant). His temporal range of vision stretched from creation to the final judgment and eternal kingdom.

Unfortunately, as Christopher Lasch has noted, we live in a culture characterized by "the waning of the sense of historical time."[5] In advertising, popular culture and the psychotherapeutic guild, people are encouraged to get it all, and get it now. Our culture is fundamentally existentialist: it tells us to live for this moment. Despite the passing fad a few years ago of exploring one's family roots, we are ignorant of our particular stories, our culture is basically uprooted, substantially irresponsible and uncaring about the future.

Technique works by abstracting situations from their past: its predictive powers have an extremely limited range into the future. But personal (and cultural) meaning is related to purpose, development, progress and movement from one point in time toward purposeful goals at another point. Christian ethicist Stanley Hauerwas has recently stressed the importance of *story* and narrative for our life.[6] For Christians, the history of decades and centuries is important; but so too is the broader trajectory wherein God's purposes in creation, as well as the revelation of the coming kingdom, bear on the meaning and conduct of our present.

The Christian urban sociologist will, therefore, want to introduce historical perspectives, long- and short-range, into his analyses. And he will become familiar with the biblical history of cities and their relation to God for illumination of today's programs and decisions. An attorney will not limit her perspectives to today's legal technicalities but will become historically informed, studying the history of Israel's law, Jesus' interpretation, Paul's commentary and so on. Ellen, Bill and Debbie will want to become familiar with the rich history of Christian thought and experience in financial matters (the medieval debates about usury, for example), healing and health care, and education. Stan's electronics field is new but there are Christian reflections on technology, its cultural and theological significance going back to the Industrial Revolution.

A deep historical mind: the second mark of a Christian mind.

A Humanist Mind

The third expansion and focusing of a Christian mind goes beyond mere abstract facts, studies, theories and knowledge; it goes beyond selfish narcissism, beyond impersonal or predatory relationships, to a deep concern for persons. "Even the very hairs of your head are all numbered. So don't be afraid; you are worth more than many sparrows" (Mt 10:30-31). In this sample text Jesus illustrates the incredible value of human life. *Humanism* has become a negative term in our era because of its association with secularism and the associated deification of the creature in place of the Creator. *Christian humanism*, however, has a much longer history than any other variety and expresses a crucial concern of biblical Christianity. The humanist movement of a Christian mind *follows* (rather than precedes) the theological movement and is actually a product of that first movement. It is God who insists that we be Christian *humanists*.

Left to itself, the mind is easily reduced to a tool for the domination of nature, society and other people. Abstraction, specialization and impersonalization can all become dehumanizing. People become face-less statistics. The speed, complexity and competitiveness of modern life make personal concern difficult. Our neighbors, clients, students, patients and colleagues remain substantially anonymous. Left to itself, the mind inclines toward care for the self above all others.

Jesus, as in the text quoted above, displayed continual concern for persons, their needs, relationships and possibilities. His concern for women (in a sexist situation), for Samaritans (in a racist situation), for children, the hungry and poor stunned his contemporaries. Note well that this is the same Jesus who lived so deeply and persistently in relation to God. Biblically, all people are created in the image of God and are the objects of Jesus' redemptive death. They are of extraordinary value.

A robust biblical humanism will be concerned for *all* persons near and far, including the poor, the outcast, those with no voice, the weak and undesirable (and not only with the popular poor). It will be concerned with whole persons, including their minds, souls and spirits as well as bodies, their dignity and history, and their interpersonal and environ-mental relationships. For an urban sociologist the city is the habitation of people, not merely statistics, and he will keep that perspective in the forefront during any study or work. For a Christian attorney, the formal technicalities of law are subordinate to the importance of the flesh-and-blood persons she serves. Ellen's customers, Stan's clients, Bill's patients and Debbie's future students all need to loom larger than financial bottom lines or statistical productivity.

We live in an epoch of narcissistic individualism and selfishness. When we do think of people they are too often reduced to statistical abstractions and numbers.

A personally concerned, humanist mind: the third mark of a Christian mind.

An Ethical Mind

The fourth characteristic of a Christian mind is its ethical sensitivity to good and evil. "Hate what is evil; cling to what is good. . . . Do not be overcome by evil, but overcome evil with good" (Rom 12:9, 21). The sort of moral passion evidenced in St. Paul's statement to the Roman Christians is not characteristic of the modern mind. Despite occasional flurries of moral rhetoric (usually directed to distant enemies like South Africa), much of our business and academic world seeks value-neutrality. Facts are distinguished, as much as possible, from values. Facts are the truly important subject matter in an advanced scientific era. Values are considered relative—to communities if not more often simply to individuals. In their most extreme form, good and evil are viewed as purely emotive statements of personal preference. Short of a philosophical commitment to this position, many people are nevertheless inclined to view many sectors and questions of life as ethically neutral.

A Christian mind does not press an immediate value judgment on every fact because (as a historical and humanist mind) it knows that facts themselves are not isolated but located in a web of other facts over a period of time. Still, any suspension of ethical judgment is for a Christian mind only temporary, for facts are laden with values and must be located in a context of ethical response. From the Creator's first pronouncement of the good to the final judgment between good and evil, the Bible illuminates and forms the Christian ethical mind. Jesus, sometimes gently, sometimes loudly, speaks and acts for good and against evil. No matter how thorny and difficult the application may be, the Christian mind has a persisting ethical sensitivity and passion rooted in God's character and Word.

Part of the Christian perspective on ethics is that God's moral standards are absolute and permanent insofar as they reflect his character and are identified as ongoing standards and virtues in Scripture. A true ethical mind is also conscious of the richness and complexity of the biblical revelation on ethics. It knows that good and evil are not merely phenomena of individual life but also must be understood in their corporate and structural dimensions. The ethical mind absorbs the *content* of biblical morality, and it learns the biblical *method* of individual and corporate discernment and action in ethics.

A Christian computer expert like Stan may not be able to pass immediate judgment on a new program design; eventually, however, he must seriously reflect on whether this program, when marketed and applied, will likely contribute to God's good purposes for human life or not. Any historian might study the rise and impact of Hitler and the Third Reich; but a Christian historian is bound to note the presence and power of evil as well as the good which rose against it. It cannot remain a neutral curiosity. A Christian psychologist cannot be content with a disinterested, value-free analysis of why a husband is beating up his wife; the psychologist must "hate what is evil," designate it as such and assist her clients in "overcoming evil with good." Our urban sociologist cannot be content with cataloging statistics on homelessness, poverty or unemployment without passing ethical judgment and promoting an ethically good response. In banking, medicine and education, Ellen, Bill and Debbie will be confronted by difficult ethical issues almost every day. As Christians, they have the resources to identify these problems and constructively contribute to their resolution.

A passionate, sensitive, ethical mind: the fourth mark of a Christian mind.

A Truthful Mind
The fifth characteristic of a Christian mind is its commitment to truth.

Jesus said, "I am the way and the truth and the life" (Jn 14:6). "You will know the truth, and the truth will set you free" (Jn 8:32). In our era, the meaning of truth has undergone a twofold reduction. On the one hand it refers to accurate, scientifically verifiable descriptions of facts; on the other hand, it refers to the authenticity with which you share your personal opinions. "It's true for me," we learn to say. A Christian view of truth goes well beyond these notions.

Although there are subjective, personal and transient aspects to some truths, Christians also affirm the existence and importance of objective truth, truth which is true whether everyone accepts it or not, truth which is defined by its correspondence with an objective reality, whether that reality is popular or not.

Second, truth in a Christian view implies a certain relationship and responsibility on the part of the knower. There is a subjective relationship between the knower and the known. This subjective relationship does not mean that truth can be defined however one wishes (because truth is controlled by its object); rather, it means the knower has a responsibility to act on what he or she knows to be true. The Hebrew term *yada* ("to know"), used for sexual intercourse as well as other kinds of knowing, implies just this sort of engagement and participation. A scientist with a Christian mind accepts responsibility for opening Pandora's box, and cannot recklessly plunge ahead with research, pawning off all responsibility on politicians and others for what use is made of his or her work. An urban sociologist must respond to what he knows to be true about a given situation or problem; an attorney must act on what she knows to be the truth in a given legal situation. Knowledge of the truth brings responsibility.

The third aspect of truth for a Christian mind is its unity. In an age of minute specialization, many modern people, frustrated by the speed and complexity of life, do not pursue a unified, integrated world view. But a Christian mind believes that God's creation has a wholeness, integrity and unity that repays our efforts to understand it. So, too, Christians are convinced that in the coming kingdom God will "bring all things in heaven and on earth together under one head, even Christ"

(Eph 1:10). Thus, the unity of truth will elude us if we merely try to fit various pieces of the puzzle together on our own. Jesus Christ is *the Truth* in whom all partial truths find their unity. A Christian mind strives to know the truth in and of Jesus Christ, and then relate everything to him. This means concretely that even the truth of the city, or of law and justice, or of money, or any other subject, can only be grasped as a whole when Jesus Christ's relations to those phenomena are understood. "If you hold to my teaching, . . . then you will know the truth, and the truth will set you free" (Jn 8:31-32).

Fourth, a Christian mind knows that truth is finally not abstract correspondence with facts alone but is a living person: Jesus Christ. The truth is alive and has power to set people free. A Christian mind means trust in Jesus Christ, cultivating a personal relationship with this living truth.

For Ellen, Stan, Bill and Debbie, the implications are fairly obvious. The facts of their respective professional lives must be related to the great Fact of Jesus Christ. And what they discover to be true carries with it an obligation to act responsibly. They cannot beg off responsibility for what they know.

A free, responsible truthful mind: the fifth mark of a Christian mind.

An Aesthetic Mind

The sixth mark of a Christian mind is its aesthetic orientation. "Whatever is lovely, whatever is admirable . . . think about such things" (Phil 4:8). "The LORD God made . . . trees that were pleasing to the eye and good for food" (Gen 2:9). In our world, the emphasis is on what things are "good for." "Pleasing to the eye" is a quality sometimes considered but usually because it makes something "good for" business. Remember that Jesus, too, was concerned not only with what was good, true and useful, but with beauty, like the lilies of the field.

The pressure of modern life and the utilitarian prejudice of our technological stress on efficiency and the bottom line have led to a great deal of ugliness. Among Christians it has mistakenly been assumed that it is more spiritual to be austere and ascetic (though we are remarkably inconsistent in this). But extravagant aestheticism is to beauty what arid intellectualism is to truth and knowledge. What is needed is balance and unity in our minds and lives. I am not suggesting that Christians become a class of impractical aesthetes or cultured snobs but that we make a significant place in our thinking for creating and enjoying beauty.

The impoverishment of our poetic and artistic sensibilities impinges on our capacity to worship, play, care for the environment and other people, and even our ability to reason. A Christian mind must be attuned to the beautiful as well as the true and the good. An urban sociologist or city planner will pay attention to beauty in the city and the lives of its citizens. So, too, attorneys, homemakers, computer programmers, bank executives, doctors, teachers and everyone else will resist captivity only to the technicalities of their fields and will find ways to promote and enhance the aesthetic elements as well.

A beauty-promoting aesthetic mind: the sixth mark of a Christian mind.

The Joy of a Christian Mind

In varying degrees, each of the above six characteristics might be part of your education. Non-Christians are often interested in one or more of these factors, and we can appreciate and learn from their efforts. Sometimes they put Christians to shame in one or another of these domains. In general, however, our techno-pluralistic world and its universities do not produce minds with these characteristics. Even the classic philosophers (who were deeply interested, for example, in the Good, the True and the Beautiful) were missing some crucial components. The whole of Scripture calls us to these characteristics; Jesus Christ calls his disciples to these marks.

I will return in later chapters to specific proposals for how to acquire these characteristics. Though difficult, it is possible for each of us to embark on this adventure with confident hope. No one arrives at full conformity to the mind of Christ in this life. But the journey even in this life is filled with meaning and understanding, companionship and growth—in a way and to a degree that serving as a cog in the techno-system can never provide. It's like playing real baseball instead of stick ball!

Pervading each of the six movements should be a deep, unquenchable experience of joy. "I have told you this so that my joy may be in you and that your joy may be complete" (Jn 15:11). "The kingdom of God is . . . righteousness, peace and joy in the Holy Spirit" (Rom 14:17). "The fruit of the Spirit is love, joy, peace . . ." (Gal 5:22). The call to a Christian mind is not a dull, dry, dusty obligation to become some kind of intellectual! It is a joyful adventure in growth. True, we are commanded to love God with our mind. But that command is enclosed within a much bigger promise and gift: you are *invited* to launch out on a great, true adventure with God and your brothers and sisters by your side.

For Reflection and Discussion

1. Which of the six marks of a Christian mind are the most exciting challenge in your studies or work right now?

2. Which one seems like the greatest challenge for you now in your development of a Christian mind?

3. Is the list complete? Are there other marks of a Christian mind that should be added, like peace, love, righteousness, or are these included within the six listed?

4. How do you feel as you contemplate working on the formation of a more Christian mind? Fearful? Enthusiastic? Confused? Determined?

Notes

[1]See Harry Blamires, *The Christian Mind: How Should a Christian Think?* (London: SPCK, 1963; Ann Arbor, Mich.: Servant Books, 1978); Arthur Holmes, *Contours of a World View* (Grand Rapids, Mich.: Eerdmans, 1983). Two other fine essays on forming a Christian mind are Oliver Barclay, *The Intellect and Beyond* (Grand Rapids, Mich.: Zondervan, 1985) and Brian J. Walsh and J. Richard Middleton, *The Transforming Vision: Shaping a Christian World View* (Downers Grove, Ill.: InterVarsity Press, 1984).

[2]Allan Bloom, *The Closing of the American Mind* (New York: Simon and Schuster, 1987), p. 41. The kind of indifferent openness Bloom describes leads to closed

minds because it is actually a relativistic avoidance of truth in any manifestation.

[3]Stephen V. Monsma, ed., *Responsible Technology* (Grand Rapids, Mich.: Eerdmans, 1986) is an excellent resource for engineers and technicians who wish to think Christianly about their work.

[4]Oscar Cullmann, *Christ and Time* (Philadelphia: Westminster Press, 1952).

[5]Christopher Lasch, *The Culture of Narcissism* (New York: Norton, 1978), pp. 3-7.

[6]For example, Stanley Hauerwas, *A Community of Character* (South Bend, Ind.: Notre Dame, 1981).

THE
CHRISTIAN
MIND
•AT WORK•
5

W*e spend a huge part of our lives working—at least half of our waking* hours, at least forty hours per week for at least forty years. For many of us, even this is a rather conservative description. I started working by mowing lawns and delivering newspapers by age ten; in high school I worked at a gas station full-time every summer and twelve to eighteen hours per week during the school year; in college I worked in a factory sixty or more hours per week every summer and most school vacations. At this stage I would guess that I work about fifty or sixty hours per week. I mention these figures because most of my friends, colleagues and family members tell the same story. We are not workaholics; this is just the way life is. Sometimes it is fun and rewarding; sometimes it is a toilsome drag.

In any case, if the Christian mind (and, more generally, Christian discipleship) doesn't apply to our work life, we are betraying Jesus' claim to be Lord of our whole life (to put it negatively) and we are losing out on an awesome adventure with Jesus (to put it positively). At work we exercise not only our bodies but our minds in the interests of our employer. We are contributing our gifts and our God-given abilities to make something happen in the world. We must not do this with blindfolds on, with our Christianity checked at the door when we arrive.

Of course, the story of our work hardly begins with our employment history. Our schooling is also focused on preparation for a job (and is itself a kind of job!). Twelve years of primary and secondary school, four or five years as an undergraduate, several more as a graduate, perhaps: and most of it is explicitly to give us training and skills for our work career. For this reason, students need to think Christianly about work as early as possible during their education. Choices a student makes as a lower-division undergraduate can have crucial influence on his or her work possibilities after university.

There is a real ambivalence about work in our society. On the one hand, often because of an absence of other sources of meaning for life, many people become workaholics, obsessively committed to their jobs. They are fidgety when not working, put in too many hours, sometimes moonlight on second jobs, and aggressively pursue success at work.

Icebreaker social questions are, "What do you do [for a job]?" and, "Where do you work?" Our jobs define our identities. The roots of this overly positive attitude toward work are multiple. Part of it is the drive toward affluence, consumerism and materialism: hard work brings more possessions. Part of it is the search for personal meaning and value. And part of it is a tradition of exalting the value of work both in capitalist and socialist societies.

On the other hand, we've all heard the phrase, "Thank God It's Friday!" Alongside the workaholics there are large numbers of people who detest their jobs and work purely out of necessity.[1] Sometimes this results in grudging, low-quality, low-productivity performance and generally negative relationships on the job. On other occasions one merely plods along or muddles through the days, waiting for weekends, vacations and retirement. Much modern work (in offices as well as factories) is monotonous, boring, toilsome, insulting, tedious and dehumanizing. (I've experienced this at times even in my best jobs!)

But there is another way, far better and more interesting than becoming a workaholic or a thank-God-it's-Friday type! This third way is to develop a Christian mind in relation to our work and career. Our challenge is to think theologically, historically, humanistically, ethically, truthfully and aesthetically about our work.[2]

Choosing a Major Field and a Job

How do most of us wind up choosing one academic major over another? How do we eventually choose certain jobs and employers rather than others? Certainly it is not completely a matter of choice. Our backgrounds, temperaments and native abilities define certain limits within which we have choices. Our family responsibilities, finances and health dictate other limits. And the job market has a lot to do with our freedom to choose.

Ordinarily, though, there are two basic criteria employed in the choice of an academic major and then a job. First, the prospects for personal fulfillment, accomplishment and enjoyment are evaluated by vocational aptitude tests and related counseling. Sometimes this is an informal process where we note the subjects we have done best in and enjoyed most, the course and major offerings that look most appealing in the college catalog, and the jobs out there that look most interesting. This is the main reason my friend Stan ended up in computers. He was brilliant in his math and science courses and has loved computers since he first discovered them in high school. He felt no need or desire to take over his parents' neighborhood grocery store. Second, we look hard at the financial prospects: Will this job be financially rewarding? Where can I make a good salary? While she is not at all characterized by greed, my friend Ellen wound up in banking largely because of the financial promise. Ellen, by the way, is the first woman in her family to work outside the home, as far as she knows, since the Industrial Revolution began two centuries ago! (Prior to that time, of course, many, if not most, married women worked alongside their husbands in small family-run businesses; the radical division between child-rearing and other work is a relatively modern invention.)

Historically, as we have noted, things were simpler. People ordinarily went into the same jobs as their parents before them. This is what my friend Bill did, following in the footsteps of his physician father. To the extent that choice was possible, family and social class decided whether you would go to certain schools and then enter certain professions or others. So despite the confusion and uncertainty of our situation, we can thank God that so many possibilities are open to us today. Debbie and Stan are both the first college-educated members of their families! Thanksgiving for *choice* seems appropriately our first Christian response.

But much more can be said about these choices when we begin to think Christianly about them. First, all of our choices in life are enclosed within two other big decisions. One of these is *our* decision to follow Jesus Christ as Savior, Lord and God. Any career decision must be integrated into that discipleship decision which claims the whole of our life.

The other decision is God's *calling* of each of his followers. Each of us has a calling (or *vocation*, to use the classic term) as a gift from God. This calling includes within it marriage or singleness, where we live, and our job. We discern this calling with the help of the Holy Spirit living within us and within other brothers and sisters who help us figure out our gifts, abilities and decisions. Theologians debate the extent to which this calling is flexible or changeable. I'm not much persuaded by hardline views ("God has your spouse, house and employer picked out for you from the foundation of the world"). But I have no doubt that all of these decisions should be made in the context of a search for God's guidance. What are your spiritual gifts? What are the general contours and directions of the life God has called you to? What is your life story all about? These are the big questions within which your choice of an academic major, and later, an employer, need to be placed.

Our understanding of and choice of work is illuminated and guided in Scripture by God's teaching and God's example. We are *taught* (or commanded) to work with our companions (a) to care for the earth as stewards of God's possession (Gen 1:28; 2:15), (b) to provide for food and the necessities of life for ourselves and our households (Gen 3:17-19; 1 Tim 5:8), and (c) to be able to give to those in need (Eph 4:28). The Bible teaches us to work to gain enough for a decent life but warns against striving to be wealthy (1 Tim 6:6-10). But we are also created in God's image and being remolded toward the image of God's Son: God the Father and Son are our examples (models) for work as in other areas. God's work produced things creative, pleasing to the eyes, useful, good and liberating. God's work was interrupted by a Sabbath for joyful rest. God's continuing work as Providence preserves life in the face of sin and disorder. His redemptive work in Jesus Christ sets people free, heals them, feeds the hungry, proclaims truthful good news and manifests loving servanthood. Our calling is to "always give [ourselves] fully to the work of the Lord" (1 Cor 15:58).

In choosing a major, a profession and an employer, our criteria should be those in the preceding paragraph. In what field (or working for what company) can I best use my abilities to be creative for life, care for God's creation, set people free, meet people's needs, speak the truth? Then we need to ask some other questions: How will this work relate to the other aspects of my calling? Will I have time for God, family, church, my neighbors?[3] Among my four friends, Debbie stands out in her quest to find a vocation with which to serve God and neighbors. School teacher or attorney? The issue for her is where God wants to use her. And although Bill seemed headed toward medical school because of family tradition, he is genuinely committed to using his training to serve God. What this approach to developing a Christian mind on the job requires is theological mind, a mind that is continually improving in knowledge of the Word of God, that is fully committed to the prayer, "thy will be done on earth as it is in heaven."

Let me finally suggest four very practical questions to ask yourself and to discuss with a few close friends who can assist your decision about what field to get into. First, "what do I really *want* to do?" As your values and desires are shaped and reshaped by the Word and will of God, there is real value in starting with this question. Within the general agenda outlined above, God plants the will within us to do his will—most of the time, anyway!

Second, "what have I already been doing?" Few people, for example, who want to serve God by being a reporter or a writer can really stifle the gift. They find avenues to report and write. And few who are called to teach or administer can hide it. Have you already been an organizer or taught classes? A pattern usually emerges even by age twenty that is helpful in detecting what our vocation is or ought to be. (But careful! there are exceptions.)

Third, "what have other people asked me to do?" If you were asked once to teach a class or organize a project or something else—but never again—it might be that others simply don't see those gifts and abilities in your life. There are always cases where one's gifts and calling are not at all evident until later in life, so these are by no means absolute guidelines. But I would suggest that the best way to find out if you should be a teacher, for example, is to find some place to try it out now. See how you like it and whether others begin asking you to do more.

Fourth, "what will suffer most if I don't do it?" You might be a great teacher and a very good small business administrator, let us say. But it might be that there are plenty of good teachers who will fill any spot you decide not to take—whereas the small business you might run could provide jobs and services desperately needed in your community. To restate this question positively, "where (what field, what company) can I have the greatest impact for the kingdom of God?" The kingdom or rule of God, I remind you, means food for the hungry, peace for the strife-torn, and so on. It does not mean that we necessarily work for a missionary organization or a church (though that is always possible also). My friends Ellen, Bill and Stan need to periodically assess their job location. Maybe part of their career could be given to an organization that is more service-oriented than profit-oriented.

In short, the first decisions we make with regard to choosing an academic major and later a job and employer are crucial for the practice of developing a Christian mind. It is never too late to re-evaluate our situation, of course. But we may regret the years we spend following the world's decision-making patterns.

Education for Work

After we make choices about an academic major we are then channeled into a program of coursework preparing us for our eventual job. Later, when we begin the job itself, we receive additional orientation and training by peers and administrators and sometimes by continuing education institutes and seminars. We also read the leading books and journals in our area. So far as all this goes, Christians need to study and acquire competence in their fields. There is no substitute for it.

But as I have been arguing, a Christian mind requires that we "take captive every thought to make it obedient to Christ" (2 Cor 10:5). In many cases this will mean supplementing our education with additional perspectives—studying the ethics or history of our area, for example. In other cases it will mean allowing the Word of God to challenge some assumptions or conclusions in our area. All attorneys, for example, must learn well the contemporary understanding of justice; but *Christians* in law school or practice must allow that understanding to be qualified and revised by what God has to say about justice. We will need to find additional professional literature giving Christian perspectives on our field; and we will need to find other Christians in our field with whom we can explore the great issues of faith and work. In the chapters to follow, I will have some further suggestions about this lifelong educational process.

Working

Finally, we go to work, hopefully having made thoughtful Christian choices about our occupations and having aggressively developed a Christian mind during our education. Ordinarily, however, we soon find that our company is driven by technical logic, the quest for profits, success and productivity. Its practices and policies are bounded by market considerations, on the one hand, and the dictates of the law, on the other (though this is not always the case, as we often see). The company will also have a history and a culture of (often unarticulated) values and assumptions that govern its operations. Personnel at all levels will have their own values, goals, habits and perspectives that affect operations. And there you are, right in the middle of it all!

Just like any other new employees, Christians can't expect to walk in, call a staff meeting and proclaim the way of the Lord for the business! We have to win the right to be heard and it will require time, patience and quality performance before we can affect much of the company's working operations. Soon enough, however, a Christian can begin to act as a conscience for the company or organization, recalling it at least to its own highest aspirations and rhetoric. Ellen has dug up the corporate ethics statement of her bank and has initiated some informal discussions among her fellow executives along these lines. Sometimes we can act as reconcilers of adversaries within the company, sometimes between customers or clients and the company. We might be able to initiate (or support) Bible studies or fellowship groups. Stan is trying to start such a group now in Silicon Valley. Co-workers can be cared for as total human beings, including concern for families and other relationships. We can show hospitality and invite co-workers into our homes. In time, perhaps in league with other Christians, we can humbly, creatively work to more precisely direct our company toward the products and services which best conform to God's agenda for human work.

What a bore just to passively merge into some company's operations without rocking the boat when we could be pursuing the never-ending adventure of developing a Christian mind on the job, working as ambassadors for Christ (2 Cor 5:20)!

The Payoff

We go to work, we make money. Of course, it is crucial that Christians not view the paycheck as the only product of their labor. The services we provide, the products we manufacture—these are the primary vehicle of the meaning and value of our work. How do they contribute to or detract from God's work in the world? We need to resist wage-slavery and its prejudices! An unsalaried homemaker or a volunteer worker may be just as significantly (or insignificantly) working within the call of God. (The most insulting thing that homemakers have to put up with is the frequent question, "Do you work?" As the bumper sticker says, "Every mother is a working mother!") Christians need to resist the worldly notion that a paycheck is an index of the reality and value of work.

Still, money is a common result of working! A Christian mind insists that we think theologically, historically, humanistically, ethically, truth-fully and aesthetically in relation to money as well. We are part of a very wealthy civilization and must take responsibility for our material situation. The starting point, I believe, is acknowledging the fact that God alone has absolute property rights—and we are commissioned to be the stewards of his property. Money is the ordinary means by which our stewardship is extended, whether by renting or buying things. The biblical guidelines are that we are not to steal, covertly or overtly. We are not to unjustly take money—or property—by filching, or by turning in a performance or product not worth the money we are accepting for it. Nor must we be ruled by greed and covetousness in acquiring money and property.[4]

Beyond those limits, there may be a place and time for wealth in some circumstances. We must *have* in order to *give*, in any case. Paul knew how to abound materially as well as to be abased (Phil 4:12). There are many examples of wealthy followers of the Lord in the Bible. However, the Bible also cautions that life is more than the abundance of possessions we accumulate (Lk 12:15). Wealth can cause anxiety which frustrates Christian growth and spirituality (Mt 6:25-34). It can become a god (Mammon) tyrannizing its worshipers and separating them from the true God (Mt 6:24). In any case, prosperity brings with it heavy responsibilities to be rich in good works and generous (Lk 12:48; 1 Tim 6:17-19).

Bill has been exemplary in this regard. Even during very difficult financial times in medical school he and his wife have insisted on giving away a tenth of their income. Ellen and Stan have not thought about tithing until recently, since their churches stress the Christian's freedom from the law. Only in recent months have they begun to think that this freedom might mean freedom to do *more* than what the Old Testament law required, rather than less!

While it is true that God shows a special care and concern for the poor (and thus so should his followers), voluntary poverty is legitimate only if it is not the result of laziness, an occasion for pride and covetousness, or an excuse for not caring for our household and other responsibilities. So you may be (or become) wealthy, but a Christian mind does not allow that to be your life goal. And you may be poor, though that has its perils also, not the least of which is self-righteousness. It seems to me that the Bible commends simplicity and contentment as the best way of all (Prov 30:8-9; Phil 4:11-13; 1 Tim 6:6-12; Lk 12:22-34; Mt 6:19-21). In all cases generosity is the rule, beginning with the freedom we have to exceed the Old Testament principle of giving a tithe, ten per cent of all we have.

These brief reflections on the Christian mind at work (and on the way to the bank) are by no means comprehensive. But they are intended to stimulate your thinking about the exercise of developing a Christian mind in perhaps the dominant sector of your personal history. Christians will work out these issues in considerable conflict with our narcissistic, consumer society. The good news is that the resolution of this conflict in favor of a Christian mind leads to a better, richer, deeper, more meaningful vocational and financial life.

For Reflection and Discussion

1. How did you choose your academic major and/or your job and company? Who or what influenced you in this choice?

2. What are the main challenges to a Christian mind that you have encountered in your work?

3. What are your views on responsible, faithful Christian use of money and property?

Notes

[1] My former colleague Don Tinder was the one who brought this strange contradiction of workaholism and the TGIF mentality to my attention a few years ago.

[2] Arthur Holmes, *Contours of a World View* (Grand Rapids, Mich.: Eerdmans, 1983), pp. 214ff., and Oliver Barclay, *The Intellect and Beyond* (Grand Rapids, Mich.: Zondervan, 1985), pp. 101ff, also try to show how the Christian mind looks at work. John A. Bernbaum and Simon M. Steer, *Why Work? Careers and Employment in Biblical Perspective* (Grand Rapids, Mich.: Baker, 1986) is an excellent study with a good list of further books and resources for those wishing to pursue the topic.

[3] My colleague Bernard T. Adeney developed a great list of such questions, published in *Radix Magazine*, (Jan-Feb 1984) pp. 16-17.

[4] See Jacques Ellul, *Money and Power* (Downers Grove, Ill.: InterVarsity Press, 1984).

ENVIRONMENTAL REQUIREMENTS FOR CHRISTIAN •MINDS•

6

Developing a Christian mind is our response to the command and invitation of God. Our minds face special challenges today because of the pluralistic surface and the technological infrastructure of our society. Today's university is no longer capable of, or intent on, nurturing Christian minds, though it continues to provide great opportunities for specialized knowledge and skill. The basic contours of a Christian mind can be defined in reference to God, history, persons, ethics, truth and beauty. Work, as the dominant sector of our lives, is the central arena for the practical application of the Christian mind.

I have tried to stress throughout this discussion that developing a Christian mind does not produce armchair intellectuals or rationalistic eggheads. For example, there is no truly ethical mind without passionate concern, and there is no adequately truthful mind without responsibility and engagement. Still, even with this broad definition of mind, the Christian life is more than the pursuit and exercise of a certain kind of mind. To put it even more strongly, it is *impossible* to develop a Christian mind *except* in a certain kind of environment. Before turning to the curriculum for developing a Christian mind, with the six marks discussed in chapter four, we must look at the basic elements in this environment.

Time and Lifestyle

Probably the first environmental aspect we need to explore is our relationship to *time*.[1] For some people, too much time may lead to boredom, laziness and apathy. "Killing time" is an activity some of us indulge in.

Far more common, however, is the problem of too little time. Most of us struggle with a frantic pace and far too many things to do in the time allowed. We feel like we are continually running late and are behind. We increase our speed but don't catch up. As I mentioned earlier, our lives are no longer bounded or defined by nature or culture. We don't allow darkness, bad weather, or distance to stop or slow down our activities. Our society, and its laws and customs, does not insist that everything close down on weekends or holidays. If anything, people are applauded for exceeding all these traditional and natural limitations. The materialism worshiped by our culture motivates us to unbounded competitiveness. Our culture's technological advances enable such frantic activity.

Josef Pieper's classic essay, *Leisure: The Basis of Culture,* argues against our world of "planned diligence" and "total labor" wherein we no longer work to live but live to work. The original word for leisure was *skole* (Greek) or *scola* (Latin), from which we get our English word "school." Leisure did not mean idleness or empty time but a state of mind, an attitude of openness to God and the world. At its heart are contemplation, festival and worship. Human culture depends for its very existence on leisure, and leisure is not possible unless it has "a durable and consequently living link with the cultus, with divine worship."[2]

It is essential to seize control of our time and schedules, master our time instead of being mastered by it. Obviously the power of God's Spirit, an iron will and some brutal choices of priorities will be necessary to recover a balance and escape the tyranny of time. These are unlikely to be effective, however, without the strong basis of a biblical theology of time. God's decision was to create a natural rhythm of day and night; light was bounded by darkness, a rhythm varied only by the seasons. In the same creation, God set apart and blessed every seventh day as a day of rest (Gen 2:3). The fourth commandment insists on the observance of the Sabbath day both as celebrative rest from creative work (Ex 20:8-11) and as grateful relief from slavish work (Deut 5:12-15). Israel's annual calendar was interrupted by seven different festivals. Its longer range included the provision for a sabbatical year (every seventh year was different from the usual grind) and the Jubilee year (every fiftieth year was extraordinarily unique). Within an Israelite's life, changes in work and responsibility were coordinated with transitions at ages twenty, thirty and fifty (see Num 1:3; 4:3; 8:25).

Certainly, there is a great deal of freedom in our interpretation and application of this material (see Rom 14:5-6). But we are made out of the same stuff as the ancient Israelites. Our lives, like theirs, need to be lived out within a rhythmic, planned pattern structuring our days, weeks, years and lifetime. Lacking a cultural (or even ecclesiastical) framework for this rhythm, we will need to invent it ourselves. The crucial thing is to plan out this calendar (from daily schedule to lifetime plan) and to dedicate it to the Lord. Just as your financial tithe is where you should begin your spending, your leisure time (especially those parts explicitly centered on God) should define the space for your work, not the other way around. The only firm basis for this planning is in your encounter with God. Good intentions will not be enough to affect this pattern if you don't really meet God on a regular basis.

Matters of lifestyle and priorities are certainly related to all of this. Many of us need to unclutter our lives and reduce the number of distractions we live with. Getting rid of a television set, concentrating on three magazines instead of ten, volunteering to work on one committee at church instead of three. . . . These are some of the moves we may need to make. There is a widespread assumption that anything we can do, we should do; anything we can afford, we should buy. It's a lie.

Too many of us lead chaotic, frenzied existences. There will be periods of time when an all-nighter is necessary, when grueling, sacrificial effort takes us to our limits, when exhaustion is reached. It may be necessary to work a weekend or two; for three or four years you may need to push yourself harder than usual. But these must be consciously chosen exceptions, not uncritically accepted manipulation by the world around you.

If this problem of time and lifestyle is not resolved, we can forget trying to develop a Christian mind.

Personal Wholeness

There is a sad irony in the fact that our society can be characterized as individualistic, self-centered and even narcissistic—and still we see incredible conformism and epidemic self-doubt. The search for a healthy self has not worked. The self needs to be centered on its Creator. As Pascal said, there is a "God-shaped vacuum in every human heart." Nothing else can occupy the center of a healthy, whole person. And as Josef Pieper said, worship of God must be at the core of our leisure or it will disintegrate.

It is essential that we cultivate a living relationship with God.[3] As in all relationships, conversation and quality time are the requirements. Conversation, in this case, means hearing God's voice in Holy Scripture, regularly reading the Bible with the prayer, "Lord, what do you want to say to me today?" I suspect that God also communicates to us through our dreams and thoughts and through the circumstances of our lives. Our friends send us messages by the things they do (flowers? leaving a book where we will read it? giving us the silent treatment?) as well as the things they say. Only in what they say can we be certain that we understand, but their actions matter too. So too with God: only the written Word of God is decisive in what God says to us, but he speaks in other ways as well. We need to give specific, regular time to reading the Bible but we need also to "practice the presence of God," to cultivate eyes and ears for the messages God might wish to give us in addition to what we hear in Scripture.

And we need to speak. Prayer is our term for talking with God. As in other conversations, this means thanking him for things, praising him, asking questions, requesting help and even complaining. No friendship can be sustained in this world without enough conversation. Do we think our friendship with God can grow without it?

There are many possible approaches to the cultivation of friendship with God. Some highly disciplined stalwarts have risen for one or more hours of quiet time with God at 6 A.M. every day of their adult lives. For others, that time is easier to find at lunch or in the evening. Some do a little every day and a lot on weekends. The point is that it must be a priority in our lives to schedule such quality time with God. Richard Foster describes how we can cultivate personal spiritual depth through prayer, meditation, fasting, study and other disciplines. Journal-keeping and other techniques can help us grow toward personal health and wholeness.

There is still more, however, than spiritual depth. "For physical training is of some value, but godliness has value for all things, holding promise for both the present life and the life to come" (1 Tim 4:8). The intellectual and spiritual dimensions are more important than our physical condition. But there is no doubt that diet, exercise and physical play is important to our total health. While many Americans today are part of a fitness boom, others help us lead the world in obesity, cancer and heart trouble. Especially when so many of us have relatively sedentary jobs, it is not a frill to give some regular time to exercise and to be careful about what we eat and drink. Making sure we get enough time for sleep and quiet relaxation is also crucial if we wish to be healthy.

Personal quiet time for conversation with God, regular exercise, sleep and good eating habits are often the first things to suffer under the pressures of modern life and work. When extreme demands are made on us at school or work, our energy for self-discipline is exhausted by the time we come to the table to eat or consider whether to get the sleep or exercise we know we need. The only way out of this situation is to rebuild our total schedule with adequate, regular time for these necessities. A Christian mind cannot exist in the absence of a personal walk with the living God; and it cannot thrive in the absence of efforts to keep our bodies healthy.

Family and Friends

Two of the worst casualties of our frantic, mobile existence are our families and friends. Part of the reason psychologists, therapists and counselors are doing such a booming business is that families and friendships have been weakened. We have no one to talk to in depth, no one who will listen, no one who can help us with crucial decisions, comfort, exhort or assist us. We are substantially alone, devoid of deep and long-term relationships. Our parents, brothers, sisters, grandparents, aunts and uncles are either many miles away or too busy (like we are). Our friendships tend to be shallow and short-term, shifting as we make our pilgrimage from one church to another, one neighborhood to another, one job to another, or even from one spouse to another.

In the creation accounts in Genesis, the only time God declares anything *not* good is when he says, "It is not good for the man to be alone" (Gen 2:18). As Karl Barth put it: "Humanity is co-humanity." To be fully human we require the living presence of others. It is subhuman to live an isolated existence. We need other people's gifts to supplement ours ["The eye cannot say to the hand, 'I don't need you!' " (1 Cor 12:21)]. We need to be in relationships where we can *receive* from others and where we can *give* care to others.

We need more than casual acquaintance with people in our own peer group, profession and neighborhood. But we also need meaningful relationships with those much younger and older than ourselves, with intellectuals and nonintellectuals, with members of races and social groups other than our own, with singles as well as married people, men as well as women, conservatives as well as liberals and anarchists. Obviously we cannot have deep relationships with more than a few people, but in the circles of our relationships we must recognize and alleviate the poverty of our isolated lives.

As in our relationship with God, long-term commitment, regular quality time and two-way conversation are essential. We must eat with others, play and celebrate, worship and learn together. Many of us need to rebuild (or build for the first time) our relationships with our parents, children, grandparents, nieces, nephews, cousins and other relatives. And many of us need to choose a couple of friends for long-term committed relationships. Some of us need to concentrate on becoming best friends with our spouses. And how many of us have become friends to any of our neighbors? You can make all the other motions of a Christian mind, and work hard for personal health, but you will lose in the end if you don't make family and friends a priority.

Church and Parachurch
Of only one institution is it said, "The gates of Hades will not overcome it," and that, of course, is the church (Mt 16:18). The church is the very body of Christ (Eph 1:22-23). Today the Church is the continuation of God's incarnation on earth, replacing Jesus of Nazareth who now acts as head of that body spread over the earth. All of this remains true despite the miserable condition of many parts of that church. The church exists for corporate worship, proclamation of the Word of God, and mutual care among the members. It stands as a witness to the world by both its deeds and words, and a resource for its needy neighbors. It nourishes and disciplines its members. It supports the discipleship of its members in their personal lives, households, workplaces and in society.[4]

Our relationships with local churches (and denominational traditions) are serious roots of our weakness today. Many people change churches frequently, sit as uncommitted spectators and never really join in a local body in a way that would either honor God or put them in a place to reap the fruit of churchly life. Others are run ragged by too many church meetings and committees. The problem is that our lives need to be centered on the corporate worship of God—and worship is different from running around the church building. We need to submit ourselves to the teaching and exhortation of godly pastors, and not always choose our own instructional diet. The church is also the place where cross-generational relationships and friendships can often best be found.

There is no adequate substitute for faithful church membership. Parachurch groups that draw their participants' loyalties away from the local church (even during university days) are undermining a basic Christian necessity. I agree with Howard Snyder and many others, that *church* means both large group and small group experiences.[5] We need somehow to be in a regular small group (five to fifteen members or so) where we can more personally pray, share our concerns, study, learn, celebrate and care for each other—as well as participate in the larger group worship joined by a wider cross-section of the body of Christ.

For most of us, one or two parachurch groups will also be an ongoing part of our experience. It is not possible in most churches to gather a group of attorneys for deep reflection on discipleship and work as a lawyer. In the Christian Legal Society it is. In many churches there are only one or two college students. InterVarsity Christian Fellowship and other campus groups provide support and fellowship that is essential for many of these students. So too, Christian magazines, arts groups, social service agencies, schools, institutes and other parachurch groups are important for many Christians. Some of these groups are key resources for those who wish to cultivate Christian minds in their profession or field. Provided that they do not overwhelm the other components in the environment of a Christian mind—such as the family and church—they are to be applauded and supported.

A Christian mind cannot be developed without strong and steady participation in a local church; and it might be crucial for the development of your Christian mind for you to be an active participant in a parachurch group as well.

Society and Culture

Finally, the environment of a Christian mind must include love of neighbor and responsible participation in the society and culture of our neighbors. Christian discipleship is not just between the self and God or even the church and God—or we might as well proceed to heaven immediately. We are placed in the world as ambassadors for Christ (2 Cor 5:20), as a "city on a hill" (Mt 5:14). A great deal of our responsibility for this ambassadorship is carried out on the job. But we are also part of apartment complexes, neighborhoods, cities, states, nations, the world.

One of the most important aspects of our social responsibility is *evangelism.* This means talking to people about Jesus. It is making a personal introduction of Jesus to someone who doesn't know him. No matter how much we share with people about the ideas of Jesus, the vocational implications of the Christian mind, or the joys of our church life, nothing replaces the fundamentally simple commission to intro-duce others to Jesus the living person. As with personal spiritual for-mation or devotional life, we may find many formulas and aides of varying quality addressing our task of evangelization or witnessing. It is not my task to add to these.[6] But if we are not at least occasionally sharing the basic gospel with others, we need to find ways to begin. We need to look among our family members, friends and colleagues for those with whom we can warmly share the good news of knowing Jesus Christ as Savior, Lord and God. A Christian mind is a bit hollow if we neglect the Great Commission (Mt 28:18-20).

But Jesus didn't just share the gospel with the society around him. He also spoke the truth about money, justice and other affairs of life. And more than speaking, he acted to meet the needs of the hungry, those ravaged by disease and disability, warring racial groups, and the anxiety-ridden. We recall Joseph and Daniel as examples of people of God working in the political power structures of Egypt and Babylon. My point is to remind us all that having a Christian mind does not mean focusing exclusive attention on our job or studies. To the extent that society and the political order are open to the influence of Christian salt and light, we ought to provide some of it as an act of faithfulness to God and love to our neighbors. We need to resist politicizing all of life at one extreme and the irresponsible political withdrawal that is at the other extreme. Ordinary politics is not the only avenue for expressing this presence, of course. Many opportunities exist for social and cultural presence outside of electoral politics.

In short, some kind of social responsibility ought to be part of a balanced Christian life. Without this dimension, a Christian mind will be missing an essential environmental factor.

A Rich and Balanced Life

All of the preceding may seem to have added considerably to the burden of responsibility a Christian bears—and we were already too busy! However, if we take some time to review our priorities and our schedules, we will find that we can build a balanced life including all of its essential dimensions. It will be a rich and full existence, but not a frenzied, overloaded one. Jesus is our example in this as in all things. While he sometimes put in long hours, the general impression one gets is that he maintained a calm, peaceful, balanced life. His secret was in giving the first place to his relationship with his Father and then in carrying out his priorities without getting continually distracted. He sometimes engaged in mass actions; most of the time he concentrated on a dozen people. He taught many things, notable more for their depth than their quantity.

Among our four friends, Stan is having the most difficult time resisting workaholism. Like many other people at his Silicon Valley firm, he often works far into the evening or night on some fascinating project. Generally a private sort of person anyway, he has not developed any deep, caring relationships at his church. Even his relationships with his two roommates are a bit superficial. Nor does Stan have an evangelistic or social-concern dimension to his life. He is still fairly young but is in danger of seeing his life slip away in a one-dimensional mode.

For Ellen, Bill and Debbie, the great difficulty is in finding the right balance between church, family, exercise and work. Each of them has all the right intentions, but it seems as though work or school, family and church are continually asking for more. How to decide priorities—

when to sacrifice grades or career advancement, when to ask the family or church for some patience and understanding, how to fit in the seemingly selfish matters of quiet time and physical exercise—are the questions. Only a periodic review of their commitments and priorities and some support from family and friends will get them and keep them in balance.

Developing a Christian mind takes some specific, directed attention, and we will turn to that later in more detail. But the burden of this chapter is that it is all for naught if we do not locate these efforts in the rich texture of a balanced Christian life.

For Reflection and Discussion

1. How would you describe your personal efforts to acquire spiritual depth and overall health? What has and has not worked for you? Where has there been imbalance?

2. Have you had significant community or friendship relationships with your relatives? Co-workers? Church? How have these relationships been sustained? How have they benefited you?

3. Which of these environmental factors are you lacking most? How can you change that? What will your next step be?

Notes

[1]The best book on this is Robert Banks, *The Tyranny of Time* (Downers Grove, Ill.: InterVarsity Press, 1984).

[2]Josef Pieper, *Leisure: The Basis of Culture* (New York:. Mentor Books, 1952, 1963), p. 17.

[3]Richard Foster, *Celebration of Discipline: The Path to Spiritual Growth* (San Francisco: Harper & Row, 1978) is a great place to start. I also like "old-timers" like Andrew Murray and A. W. Tozer as guides in this area.

[4]See David W. Gill, *Peter the Rock: Extraordinary Insights from an Ordinary Man* (Downers Grove, Ill.: InterVarsity Press, 1986), chapter 5, for more details on the church.

[5]Howard Snyder, *The Problem of Wineskins* (Downers Grove, Ill.: InterVarsity Press, 1975).

[6]See Rebecca Pippert, *Out of the Saltshaker* (Downers Grove, Ill.: InterVarsity Press, 1979).

STUDY LIST: THE CHRISTIAN MIND •CURRICULUM• 7

W*hat do we study to get there from here? That is the question of this* chapter. In my undergraduate days, you signed up for a series of courses and registered for these on your study list. What are the courses necessary in a curriculum for a Christian mind? In the next chapter I will discuss the question of how we can master these subjects, since they are not in most of our university catalogs!

Professional Expertise and Remedial Liberal Arts

Actually, we begin with two items that are available in most university catalogs. Professional expertise and remedial liberal arts will not by themselves make for a Christian mind; but they are essential ingredients nonetheless. The first of these is your own specific professional preparation. It is essential that Christians become excellent in their own

fields—as excellent as your God-given abilities and a balanced life
permit. We cannot all be trailblazing geniuses and career stars. But lots
of biblical knowledge in law and justice, for example, combined with
sloppy, incompetent legal preparation doth not a good Christian legal
mind make! If an impressive knowledge of biblical texts and a fervent
prophetic zeal like Amos's are combined with shallow platitudes and
historical naiveté, even the highest aspirations of a Christian journal-
istic mind will be sorrowfully undercut.

We must strive for excellence in our professional training. There is
indeed scandal and reproach connected to following Jesus Christ. But
the New Testament makes clear that this scandal is to be the cross and
resurrection, not our own stupidity or laziness. If a professor (or a
colleague) is negative or hostile to our work, it should be because of the
cross, not our ineptitude. In Paul's famous speech to the Areopagus (Acts
17:16-34), his philosophical audience burst out laughing when he
spoke about the resurrection *not* because he misquoted or misused their
ancient poets. If our director is angered because a financial report is
poorly done, or a professor rejects shoddy research and writing, no
amount of fish-pin wearing or pious platitudes will change the fact that
their reactions are justifiable and not anti-Christian prejudice.

Professional excellence brings glory to God, and it wins us the right
to be heard among our colleagues. In any case, if we wish to integrate
our Christian faith with our professional thought and work, the latter
must be of the highest possible quality. In Stan's and Bill's cases, excellence is ever-present. Ellen would not be a vice president if she were
not also a superb performer. She does, however, struggle to find time
to keep up with her field *and* the demands of her family. It is a tough
balance to find.

The second item on our list is also not specifically Christian study.
As noted in chapter three on the modern university, most of our ed-
ucations are weak in the liberal arts that acquaint us with the broad
texture of our civilization.[1] Given the biblical emphasis on history and
on the universality of God's purposes, Christians must undertake, as
necessary, remedial studies to upgrade their understanding of history,

geography, literature, the arts, politics and other fields. We need to become familiar with the great classics which have both reflected and shaped our civilization.

In our global civilization it is more important than ever to carry out some international or crosscultural studies (rather than be content with the stereotypes of television and newspaper reporting). We need to study foreign languages not only to facilitate communication crossculturally, but for the humbling and enlightening experience in itself. Nonscientists need to study some science and technology; technicians and scientists need to study history and literature. Stan is so consumed with his computer work that he has a very weak education in other areas. And yet it is especially important for people in new vocations to discern the broader cultural fabric in which they live and work.

Again, professional expertise and remedial liberal arts are not sufficient in themselves for a Christian mind. But they are, I submit, essential components in our study list on the way to that goal. I'm sure my comments on remedial liberal arts are a bit daunting. Remember, though, we are talking about a *lifetime adventure,* mastering a little more every month and year, not doing it all at once!

Biblical Studies

It will come as no surprise that the Bible is the first specifically Christian subject on our study list. The Old and New Testaments are the most crucial part of the curriculum. There can be no Christian mind without a good, growing knowledge of the written Word of God. Biblical illiteracy is a scandal not only in the world but even in the church. The decline of biblical memorization in modern churches and Sunday schools is frightening. The Bible needs to be read, studied, pondered, and reread throughout our lives. If it is true that our physics, law, history or science textbooks require careful, determined attention from cover to cover, how much more is that true of God's Word!

There are four major aspects to our biblical studies which need simultaneous attention. First, we need to become familiar with the historical backgrounds, cultural settings, authorship and purpose of each of the sixty-six books. To be sure, if God had thought it essential for us to know all of this before we could hear him speak through Scripture, he would have inspired a few prefaces on these matters to lead off each book! But it won't work to let ourselves off the hook that easily. A great deal of the introductory material to which I refer comes from careful reading of the text itself.

But God chose to give us a collection of writings from the ancient world, written by many different authors, at different times and places, in relation to different problems, by different personalities, in different styles. The original audiences did not usually need to do background studies (or linguistic translation) as we must. For us to understand and appreciate more fully Jesus' teaching and activities, for example, we need to understand the differences among the four Gospels and their authors, the historical situation of the Roman Empire, the Jewish political and religious parties to whom he spoke (Pharisees, Sadducees, and others), the nature of historical writing (and Gospel writing) in that time, and so on. A good book on Bible introduction, an annotated study Bible or various Bible commentaries, along with an Old Testament history and a New Testament history, will be invaluable for all of this.

Second, it is important to engage in a careful reading of each of the sixty-six books, learning their outline, form and specific content. We will need to take notes as we read, make outlines and even memorize certain texts that strike us as especially powerful or important. We need to note recurrent, major words and ideas that dominate individual books. Is the Revelation (Apocalypse) of John a blizzard of disconnected images in your mind? Can you describe the major sections of Paul's Letter to the Romans? Do you know the names and general content of the Book of the Twelve (the Minor Prophets)? If this is the Word of God, having the answers to such questions is important.

Third, we must try to get a handle on the unifying themes and movements in the Bible as a whole.[2] Jesus Christ is the center of this total revelation; he is the personal Word of God (Jn 1; Heb 1) within the written Word of God. The character and activity of God, the general contours of evil, the meaning of the good, truth, justice, sexuality, peace and war—these are some of these overarching topics. Some of these topics cutting through much (or all) of the canon will have special relevance and application for particular situations in our lives. Wisdom, learning and work will be acutely important for students and lay disciples. Health and related topics will be of crucial concern for healthcare professionals. Money, wealth and poverty will interest us all but especially those in financial operations and business.

Fourth, we will need to study basic principles of interpretation and application.[3] We must not have any part of a proof-texting approach that jerks phrases out of their context to support one of our interests. The basic guidelines in this area are deduced from the way the Bible interprets itself, the later authors' ways of quoting and interpreting earlier Scripture (notice the methods of Jesus and Paul). But it is complicated and there are excellent (as well as mediocre) books, articles and courses on this subject.

In carrying out this part of the curriculum we are inviting God to give us a theological mind, to bring his truth into our arena. We are inviting God to speak to us and form our minds. Our historical, humanist, ethical, truthful and aesthetic mind will also be powerfully affected at the same time we theologize it. The Bible is a long and often complex book. None of us will master it in a day or a year. The point is to get it on our study list every semester of our lifetime.

Historical and Crosscultural Studies
A Christian mind must be an historical mind, for reasons discussed in chapter four. Closely related to historical depth is crosscultural breadth. We can not live out our lives as autonomous points isolated from the past or from the multitudes outside of our personal enclave. Biblical study will add immeasurably to both historical and crosscultural perspectives. Remedial liberal studies will be invaluable. But I wish to speak particularly about Christian history from the first to the twentieth centuries, and the Christian experience outside of our habitat and culture. We are neither the first nor the only Christians to ask about faithful discipleship in the world. Those who have preceded us have much to

teach us; those struggling for faithfulness in other parts of the world are also members of the body of Christ, indispensable for our discipleship.

The problem with most church history textbooks (and courses) is that they usually focus on (a) ecclesiastical disputes and divisions, (b) dogmatic or doctrinal questions, and (c) elite leadership among the clergy. These are interesting and often important. We should acquire at least a basic awareness of Augustine, Aquinas, Luther, Calvin and the rest. (Do you know when the Reformation began, and why?) So, too, our crosscultural awareness is generally confined to information about the missionary extension of ecclesiastical bodies.

What we need, however, for Christian minds in today's workplace and university, is the social and intellectual history of our predecessors. On a general level, for instance, many Christians have grappled with the meaning of work, law, money and political reform throughout the centuries. During the fourth century, Theodosius led the attempt to remodel Rome's constitution on a Christian basis; in the sixteenth century, Calvin worked at city government as well as theological definition. In the Middle Ages people hotly disputed the morality of charging interest on loans (bankers, take note!). The Puritans' Massachusetts Bay Colony and the Quakers' Holy Experiment in Pennsylvania provide two historical models for dealing with pluralism and with violence. The church has a long history of participation in medicine and nursing (doctors and nurses, take note!). On the crosscultural level, Christians in Latin America and Africa have much to teach us about relating to corrupt political and economic forces. So, too, there is a history of Christian response to technology and of Christian participation in education and schooling.

The preceding examples are only samples. I submit that a Christian mind ought to be historically and crossculturally deepened and broadened. At times we will learn from the mistakes of our predecessors; at other times their triumphs will teach us.

Theological and Ethical Studies
Theology is the systematic summation of our understanding of God.

Ethics is the systematic reflection on the implication of theology for our daily life. These definitions are not universally accepted, but this is what I mean by the terms. Theology and ethics are two sides of the same coin. Theology is systematic discourse about God; ethics is about the good and the right. But for Christian ethics it is precisely God who is the Good and does the Right; hence the close relationship of the fields. For Christians there can be no theology without an ethics, because knowledge of God brings responsibility and possibility into the lives of those who know him. And there can be no Christian ethics without theology, because all ethics is dependent on our knowledge of and relationship to God.

It might be nice to be content simply with knowing the Bible and living in simple obedience to its instruction. But we are talking about a sixty-six book collection on the one hand and an awesomely complex modern culture, two and three millennia removed from the settings of those books, on the other. Every Christian needs to come to terms with the basic outlines of the revelation of God and have a basic doctrinal understanding. How might you describe what you believe? We cannot really know something unless we can articulate it. Furthermore, the Bible consistently tells us that our God enters into human history. That is true for our history as well as earlier epochs. Our theology must therefore be articulated in context, in our language and situation.[4] Contextual factors must always be subordinated to the clear, transhistorical character and truth of God. (For example, the biblical revelation and explanation of the truth that God is love cannot be brought under the control of today's sappy notions of love or subjective notions of God.) But contextual factors must not be eliminated, for God affirms as well as contradicts aspects of our historical and cultural situation.

In the case of both theology and ethics, the Bible provides the crucial, normative data; historical and crosscultural perspectives add essential illumination; our own particular context is the setting. Unfortunately, a good deal of contemporary theology and ethics is a wimpy reflection of our culture and its philosophical, psychological, technical and political passions. Most theological textbooks will be of limited value (some help, but not enough!).

So too, most ethics books are less than satisfactory because they are too often either dry treatises on moral logic and language or superficial lobbying for specific ethical positions on hot issues. A genuine Christian ethics will need to begin with biblical understandings of both the method and content of the moral life. With regard to *method*, it will include stress on (1) the primacy of the Word of God in Scripture and Jesus Christ, (2) the interdependent roles of the individual and the community in moral discernment and action, (3) the importance of doing ethics in full consciousness of our story from Creation and Fall through Incarnation to the Eschaton (the coming Kingdom of God, eternity), and (4) the priority of shaping moral character over preparation for decision-making in a quandary.

With regard to *content*, a Christian ethic will move from the biblical virtues, such as faith, hope, love, truth and justice, to concrete application in one's own personal, vocational and social life. It will explore the personal and structural aspects of good and evil, and it will come to terms with the tension between Christian moral convictions and the pluralism of a world not accepting those convictions. Ethics requires us to seek thorough understanding of the complexities of the situations facing us. But Christian ethics always promises to lead us to freedom and faithfulness within or beyond that burdensome complexity.

Ellen will need to explore business and economic ethics. Bill will have a lot to study in medicine and bioethics. Studies are also being done in technological and engineering ethics that will be of help to Stan. Ethical issues in public education will need to be Debbie's special concern if she follows through her plan to become a teacher. Each disciple needs to study the theology and ethics of his or her field. It's the way we invite God to have the first and last words on our life and work; it's the way we ensure that our Christian convictions are thought through in relation to the concrete circumstances of our daily existence.

Integrative and Practical Studies

Ethical studies are most immediately applicable to an active Christian mind. But our curriculum is incomplete until we take on specific projects to draw all of the threads together in an integrative whole. And this integrative whole needs to get practically applied in our daily lives or we will have pulled up short of the goal. For an attorney, then, it might be essential to prepare a paper on "A Christian Approach to Justice in the Criminal Justice System in California" by drawing together biblical studies, history, theology, crosscultural perspectives and soundings from other lawyers (Christian and not), as well as the legal literature. Then that attorney must go to work with her practice informed and shaped by this study. Even this is not the end, of course, for she will need to continually add to her stores of wisdom, knowledge and experience and, interacting with others in and outside the field, progressively refine her Christian thinking and practice in criminal law.

My friend and student Bill carried out an integrative study focused on evangelism to patients, while another Christian medical student studied financial practices among Christian doctors. Debbie, Stan and Ellen haven't done this kind of study yet but, like all disciples, they need to carry out projects drawing together the various threads of their study list and applying it all to their jobs.

In the next chapter we will explore various ways of making our way through the Christian mind curriculum. It will be hard work at times, but it also promises to be the most rewarding study you have ever undertaken!

For Reflection and Discussion

1. How is your liberal arts background? What have you studied—and what can you study now—to supplement your knowledge?

2. How much serious Bible study of the type described in this chapter, have you already done? What role does the Bible play in your weekly schedule? Where do you need to improve or hone your study habits?

3. Have you read books or taken courses on Christian history, missions or crosscultural studies, theology or ethics? How important are these subjects to you? Which topic would you like to delve into first?

Notes

[1]This is forcefully argued in E. D. Hirsch, Jr., *Cultural Literacy: What Every American Needs to Know* (Boston, Mass.: Houghton Mifflin, 1987), and Allan Bloom, *The Closing of the American Mind* (New York: Simon and Schuster, 1987).

[2]A good example of this is a book by my colleague William Dyrness, *Themes in Old Testament Theology* (Downers Grove, Ill.: InterVarsity Press, 1979).

[3]My colleague Joel B. Green has provided two excellent aides in this process: *How to Read Prophecy* (Downers Grove, Ill.: InterVarsity Press, 1984) and *How to Read the Gospels and Acts* (Downers Grove, Ill.: InterVarsity Press, 1987).

[4]See Robert Banks's fine new study, *All the Business of Life: Bringing Theology Down to Earth* (Sutherland, Australia: Albatross, 1987).

STRATEGIES FOR BUILDING A CHRISTIAN •MIND• 8

W*hat can you do to develop a Christian mind? Most discussions of a Chris-*tian mind attempt to outline the goal, but fail to give much help on how to get from here to there. Newman and Malik propose rather grand institutional strategies: form a true university, develop an internationally distinguished body of Christian scholars to monitor the university. Alternatively, the burden is placed on the Christian college, department, or individual professor engaging in self-criticism and reform. But what about us, the consumers of these products, the students and workers on the front lines? Are we limited to waiting for these institutional reforms to succeed?

Not at all. Schools, seminars, professors, books . . . there are many sources of assistance in developing Christian minds. But the burden is on each of us to make the commitment and do the job. No institution can hand you a Christian mind. I will return to a review of some possible sources of outside assistance (seminaries, colleges and others) below. Let us begin, however, with a general strategy which all of us can follow. I am going to be very specific and concrete in my suggestions. You may prefer some other strategy, and certainly the possibilities are endless. Specific, concrete steps of some type must be taken, however, or all of this Christian-mind talk will never amount to anything more than words. I also want to repeat that these are our steps; we need to pray also that God's Spirit will be fully present guiding and strengthening us throughout our efforts.

Scheduling Time for Growing a Christian Mind

The first thing that must be done in a strategy for developing a Christian mind is to *reform our schedule and our environment*. Sit down for a couple hours with paper and pen and outline your current weekly schedule and commitments. Then draw up a new schedule with the environmental components described in chapter six. Some things will almost certainly have to go. You may need to cut back your commitments to just one committee meeting per week, one small group meeting per week, one entertainment evening per week. You may need to discipline yourself to four hours of television per week, fifteen minutes on the newspaper each day, two hours per week on magazines. Each of us is different, of course, and these examples are by no means applicable to everyone, nor do they cover all the activities of our lives. My point is that unless we seize control of our schedules, we will be doomed to a life controlled by external forces. We need to learn to say *no* to others as well as to ourselves.

Unless we cut back on some things we will find no room for other activities that need to be added. Unless we develop a disciplined *pattern* for our daily and weekly life we will need to waste considerable energy deciding everything on a case-by-case basis. If you make a personal rule of one committee meeting per week, you will have considerably less difficulty resisting pressure from others (or your own fascination) to add just one more to your life.

The total environment must be right for building a Christian mind during the course of your life. This means exercise, church, friendship and personal time for prayer and spiritual growth. If we don't have a full, balanced life pattern, we will find ourselves frustrated and exhausted. Developing a Christian mind requires its own time allotment. My bold suggestion is that you *commit yourself to five to ten hours per week of explicit efforts to develop a Christian mind.* This could be one hour every evening, three evenings of two hours each time, four hours on Saturday or Sunday, or some other pattern. In addition, at least one week per year might be devoted to just this task—for example, a week-long summer course. Three weekend or Saturday seminars might be part of your schedule. Taking a whole year off at some point could change your life. More and more people (pre-career, mid-career, post-career) are doing just this. Stan and Debbie have the best chance of doing this because they are single. For Bill and Ellen, study time will need to be carefully worked out in relation to family obligations. School teachers can often use their summers for extra study. Some businesses are introducing options for their people to take sabbaticals not unlike professors take.

Before you get discouraged by what will seem to some an impossible addition to a schedule, I must say something else. Wherever possible, we should double up on the activities of our life. I see no reason, for example, why we should separate our devotional reading of the Bible from our Christian-mind Bible study (which will be a big part of the whole enterprise). Our study should never be devoid of devotion and personal interaction with the Word of God; nor should our devotional reading be a thoughtless, haphazard exercise. And if we are in a small group, why not study the subject of work or money in the Bible or read together a book that contributes to our Christian mind? If we want to make one significant contribution to our local church, how about volunteering to teach or organize a Sunday-school class on justice or organize our personal Bible study during a given period so that it is also preparation for our class at church? As part of our quality time with our spouse or best friend we could read and discuss a book together or take a class together. If we are enrolled in courses at a university, we could try to read books and do research papers not based on personal whim but on our goal of thinking Christianly (more on university study below). We may need to substitute an evening course in Christian studies for our small group for a period of ten weeks or so.

In summary: seize control of your schedule; brutally cut back where you are overcommitted; make time for all the components of a balanced Christian life, doubling up wherever possible (killing two birds with one stone); draw up a plan for your daily, weekly, yearly and lifetime existence. None of this is achieved once for all. We will need to review and revise our schedules every few months as circumstances change. Don't be utopian and totally unrealistic in your goals—and then attack yourself (or others) when you come up short. Do be ambitious. Those who reach for the stars are unlikely to come up with a handful of mud! More likely you will hit the moon, feel a little humbled that you didn't get to Mars, but feel pretty good about getting as far as you did.

Personal Study
Set goals for your study toward a Christian mind. Write down and post them in a prominent place; share them with your housemates. Stay accountable to your goals and check them off as you hit them, and revise your schedule as needed. For example, over a five-year period you could plan to study the entire Bible and read twenty books (say, three each in Bible, theology, ethics and history, and eight in supplementary fields). This would imply covering about one biblical book each month and reading one outside book every three months. It means carefully studying about five pages of Scripture per week and reading about twenty pages of other material per week. Now those goals are achievable by anyone! A balanced, sane, rewarding life can include these activities.

As an aid to your study, you should begin investing in a small *personal library*. For a couple hundred dollars (not necessarily all at once!) you can buy a couple of Bibles (to compare translations and to be able to underline and mark up at least one), one of which might be a study Bible with annotations and notes, a good Bible commentary, a Bible dictionary, a concordance (index to Scripture), a general church history textbook, a systematic theology, an introduction to Christian ethics and a dozen other volumes on your list.

In addition to your study plan and personal library you need a *personal filing system* in which to begin storing what you are learning. Even if you use a word processor or computer for your main files, I urge the purchase of a set of one-hundred file folders and a file in which to store them (even a cheap, cardboard file is better than none). On sixty-six of those folders, write the names of the individual books of the Bible. On others write "study plan and goals," "Christian mind," "Christian ethics," "church history," "systematic theology," "crosscultural studies and missions," "work," "money," "politics," "spiritual formation," "evangelism," "law" (or whatever the name of your profession might be) and so on.

It is essential to underline as you read and then summarize your reading in a set of notes. Merely reading is not aggressive enough to retain what you are studying. Store your notes in your file folders. If you use a computer, store printed-out copies of your notes in your folders. In addition, every time you find an extraordinary article on a subject in your curriculum, put that in your files. When your pastor preaches a series on, for example, Romans, put your outlines or notes from that series in your "Romans" file. All too often our exposure to Scripture (and other subjects in Christian studies) is casual, passive and thus forgotten. Pledge to yourself that that will no longer be the case with you.

Finally, your personal study needs to include reflection and articulation. For many people, keeping a journal is a way of summarizing what they are learning, and exploring its applications to their lives. For others of us, it is important to teach a class on what we are learning as a means of securing our own understanding (as well as helping our fellow students). Still others may want to write a brief article for the church newsletter (for example, "Glorifying God on the Job") or even submit something to a magazine. Lacking professors to hold us accountable for such reflection and articulation, we will need to invent our own ways of doing so.

The Christian Mind Network

The point of suggesting that we might teach a class or write an article has to do with the importance to our learning of articulating what we are studying. But it is also important to build networks with other people seeking a Christian mind. No matter who or where you are, you can find some support and fellowship in the enterprise. Even if you are part of a small or anti-intellectual church in an isolated town, you don't need to be alone. First, your housemates or at least one other friend at church might be willing to study, pray and talk through Christian mind issues with you. Even one friend will be extremely valuable. It would be nice if a half-dozen dedicated Christians in your field would eagerly join you in your quest—but that is a rare occurrence. Ellen has been fortunate in that she and her husband are in a midweek small group, connected with their church, that is full of enthusiasts for developing a Christian mind. Debbie is involved in a campus InterVarsity Christian Fellowship group that is supportive.

Second, try to find some other Christians at your place of study or work. Put up a notice or run something in a newsletter inviting formation of a Bible study group. Stan is only now beginning to find some other Christians in Silicon Valley enterprises. You don't need to be an eloquent teacher to do this. Even if you are shy and fearful, you can draw people together for a leaderless group study. To the extent you can, you might also become humorously known to your colleagues or fellow students as the philosopher or the pastor because of your quiet (or vocal!) way of steering conversations toward God and the deeper questions of ethics, truth and the meaning of your work. You could become an expert on the history of your company or field, including any formative ethical codes or statements (many companies and professions have such statements). Organize a group to study such statements and issues. If your company does not have a code of ethics, volunteer to help write one. Help write the history of your department or company or hospital. In all of these ways you will break out of the isolation of your studies and begin interacting with both Christians and non-Christians.

Third, you should join (or form) a fellowship of Christians in your field. Many national organizations already exist, have regular meetings around the country and publish newsletters, directories, bibliographies and journals.[1] Bill has been active in the Christian Medical Society. If your field is history, join the Conference on Faith and History; if nursing, join Nurses Christian Fellowship; if law, join the Christian Legal Society; and so on. Even as an undergraduate you can join these groups for a modest rate. What these groups do is link us up with others grappling with similar issues. We may discover a colleague in the same company or town. Or we may be able to initiate a friendship by correspondence. Don't waste too much time trying to reinvent the wheel! Learn from others and move beyond the point Christians in your field have already achieved.

Unfortunately, some of our pastors and churches will throw cold water on our endeavors to develop a Christian mind. Your pastor may be threatened by lay people who study theology. Your co-worshipers may be unshakably committed to an otherworldly spirituality (and this-worldly conformity). Your company may be small or devoid of social responsibility and theological interest. And, I regret to say, some organizations of Christians in a given field (some Christian business groups are notorious here) are uninterested in asking tough questions about Christianity on the job and prefer to listen only to testimonies of conversions by stars or by former alcoholics whose businesses now run big profits.[2] But if you can find even one other kindred spirit with whom to share your journey, you will be greatly assisted toward a faithful Christian mind.

Strategies for University Students

As I have suggested numerous times in this book, the quest for a Christian mind should begin before we enter the place of professional employment. I know from personal experience the pressures of student life and the antipathy of many professors toward the Christian faith. But understand this well: the working world is no different. The same pressure you experience in university exists in the generally non-Christian (if not anti-Christian) environments of business and the professions.

Paychecks and promotions are at least as big a stake as grades are in university. If we do not practice a Christian way of thinking and a balanced Christian life as undergraduate and graduate students, we are unlikely to begin when our career is launched. (Of course, it is never too late to begin, but here I am addressing those who have a chance to get started while in college.)

Thus, all of the preceding discussions on the environment of a Christian mind and all of the strategies for personal study, goal-setting and networking described earlier in this chapter apply equally to students and to working people out in the world. Some campus Christian groups will support your efforts, and your participation will be a real source of strength. The leadership of InterVarsity Christian Fellowship, for example, is explicitly committed to preparing marketplace disciples who will relate faith to work.[3]

Should Christian students argue their faith in class? Absolutely— provided it is done with grace, humor and competence. As an undergraduate at Berkeley I remember writing a terrible paper on "A Biblical View of Recreation" for a class. Not a bad idea, but I wrote a hasty, poor paper. On the other hand, my M.A. thesis at San Francisco State University was on "Contemporary Christian Philosophies of History: The Problem of God's Role." Looking back on it, I can see how it could have been better. Still, it won the respect of my committee (none of whom indicated any personal interest in Christianity) because I worked hard and did a decent job. Answering their questions during my defense was a strengthening, confidence-building experience.

Be careful not to aggressively confront your professors, especially in public! Your manners and their insecurity are at issue. Sometimes it might be important to argue against an outrageous statement about God or the Bible by a professor. Other times we need to trust the Lord that others in the class are not harmed and wait for a more appropriate opportunity. In many classes you will have opportunities to choose a topic for a research paper. My suggestion is that you piggyback your Christian interests on a study of a Christian thinker in the field. Allow this third party to be the focus of any disagreement you encounter with the professor. This might mean doing a paper on Jacques Ellul in sociology, E. F. Schumacher in economics, T. S. Eliot in literature and so on. These might be fringe, eccentric figures in the field but they have won places in scholarly discussion (which Josh McDowell, Francis Schaeffer, Billy Graham and others, for all their value in other ways, have not). What I am suggesting is that you should piggyback your scholarly work on scholars who will open the door for your work. Often these Christian figures will be historical leaders in the field whose work preceded modern skepticism. Here, too, is where your membership in a national organization of Christians in your field will help. You can write to professors on other secular university campuses who are solid scholars and strong Christians and ask for advice.

Let's get back to Debbie again. She is a sophomore, probably about to declare an English major in preparation for a public-school teaching career. She is active in her InterVarsity group on campus. What specifically can Debbie do toward developing a Christian mind? The first move is to make a habit of bringing the God she worships in the Bible study group into class with her. She must consciously determine to think, listen, analyze, study and write with this same God in charge. This may seem obvious but I contend that we have an epidemic of compartmentalization in the Christian community. So, too, when Debbie is in her InterVarsity large and small group meetings, she needs to be there as a university student. The issues and questions of her daily classroom experience need to be part of her consciousness and conversation as she enters into Bible study, prayer, worship and fellowship. In a sense she needs to bring her field with her into the Christian setting and ask God to plant in that field (and not just in her personal religious life).

Debbie also needs to build a network of support toward developing a Christian mind. She may ask the group leaders, "Who, in the Inter-Varsity group, is an English or education major? Can we get together to discuss our common concerns? Who among the alumni were majors in my field? What are their phone numbers? Does anyone know of any Christian faculty members or teaching assistants in the English or education departments? Does anyone know the address of the Conference on Christianity and Literature? Is there an association of Christians who teach in the public schools?"

In her English class work, Debbie might prefer to choose courses (and professors) which will allow her to read and interact with theologically and ethically sensitive writers such as John Milton or Walker Percy. Even if the authors are not Christian, research might be chosen which focuses on moral and spiritual-value issues in literature, or on biblical themes and allusions in a given body of work. By carefully choosing these topics and reviewing one's thinking with alumni or other Christians in the field, a great deal of integrative Christian thinking can be carried out by Debbie. If she chooses authors, problems and paper topics carefully, she will have no need to preach or become defensive in class. She can learn to guide discussions so that the literature itself raises the issues most important to her personally. This, of course, is precisely what she will need to do as a public-school teacher also; she cannot preach or bully her younger charges with the gospel. She will need to learn how to raise the great issues of life and death, good and evil, meaning and despair, in a careful, responsible way.

Other Institutional Resources
We have discussed the potential value of national or regional organizations of Christians in various fields. In addition, campus Christian organizations and local churches can assist those interested in developing Christian minds. Special classes and study or support groups can be sponsored by campus or church organizations. Pastors and campus Christian leaders can provide leadership by stressing the importance of integrated lives. Churches can include church history, theology and other classes in their programs and can build helpful library resources. Pastors and campus Christian leaders can accumulate lists of resources to help their members. Yearly conferences on "Christian Discipleship on the Job" can be worked into the schedule. In short, the local church and campus Christian group cannot usually provide specialized help for nurses, lawyers and other professionals, but they can do a great deal to

provide general support for the biblical mandate to love God with all your mind.

Or perhaps there is a Bible school or institute near where you work or study. These institutions have contributed greatly to the foreign missions movement and to their students' basic knowledge of Scripture. A course or two might be helpful as you develop your Christian mind. In general, however, Bible institutes are geared for high-school graduates and will not educate you at the same rigorous level you direct to your own professional preparation. Your fellow students may be very young and not as interested as you are in the Christian integrative mind at work. Finally, the Bible institute often is (geographically and intellectually) separated from the world of ideas and work in which you must operate. And you may not find an explicitly integrative focus because of the old prejudice that the Bible applies itself if you just learn its surface content.

Many of these comments can apply to Christian liberal arts colleges as well. The level of instruction is geared to a young student body, often sent there by parents wishing to protect them from the world. If you are fortunate enough to be able to study with Christian college scholars like Arthur Holmes of Wheaton, do it! But my general impression (from many lecture tours to Christian colleges) is that most Christian college professors are no more interested in integration than are their secular counterparts. Their courses treat economics, medicine, law, sociology, history and other fields just as they would be treated in major universities—but without the same level of academic depth and stature as the latter!

Another possibility is the theological seminary. Many of these seminaries offer excellent courses in Bible, theology and other subjects essential for a Christian mind. Some are developing programs explicitly for lay people. The seminary is a graduate-level institution, which gives your studies the rigor they need. However, the seminary is usually located far from the university and lacks a conscious intention to relate its work to that institution. And no matter how many lay programs a seminary develops, the basic thrust of seminary classes remains the preparation of pastors—as it should! A course in New Testament has got to focus on preparing students to preach sermons from the text— not apply it in one's business or law practice. David Hubbard, president of Fuller Theological Seminary, recently acknowledged that his seminary is "inclined to treat [lay people who attend] as though they're going to change professions [to become clergy]. We give them new professional training rather than fortification and reinforcement to serve Christ in their present professions."[4] His opinion is shared by most other seminary presidents I have known or heard.

Most promising as institutional supports are the growing numbers of study centers on the edges of the great universities of our time. The MacKenzie Study Center next to the University of Oregon and the Westwood Christian Foundation next to UCLA are two examples of study centers with fine resources helping Christians integrate their faith with their studies and work. Courses, conferences, a small library and a small but competent staff are available to support those seeking Christian minds. Taking advantage of such opportunities is a great idea.

Finally, in a few locations graduate schools of Christian studies for the laity have been founded next to major universities. These institutions have top-quality graduate faculties, fine libraries, master's degree programs for those who wish, part-time study programs, courses explicitly focused on lay disciples and various conferences and seminar programs throughout the year. The (Dutch Reformed) Institute for Christian Studies at the University of Toronto, Regent College (and now seminary) at the University of British Columbia, and New College Berkeley at the University of California are graduate schools of this type. Taking out a year for study at one of these schools is, in my view, the very best help you could give yourself in building a Christian mind. Studying part-time for several summer schools or in evening programs is also a great option. Attending conferences or dropping in to consult with faculty members is the least demanding relationship but still of considerable assistance to your studies.

Bill has made the costly move of spending a year in full-time study at New College Berkeley after finishing medical school. Stan has recently become a regular (one course per semester) student at New College Berkeley. Ellen has managed to fit in five courses over the past five years but was forced by her busy schedule to audit them, rather than completing credit work. What these three friends have done at New College Berkeley has been done by many other busy people like you, at many educational institutions.

So we see that there *are* ways to develop Christian minds in our busy era. The strategies and resources are available to all who make the commitment, at any age, in any region or any profession. Let me conclude by reviewing some strategies for each of our four friends.

Ellen has all the pressure of a busy family life with her husband and two high-school children. In addition she has a long, one-hour commute each morning and evening. Still, Ellen can buy the file folders and a basic library as I mentioned earlier. Instead of driving to work she could take public transportation and use that two hours per day for reading and prayer (ten hours per week!). With her family, she could pledge to read the whole Bible over a three- to five-year period, taking thirty minutes after each session to add to her own notes in her files. As noted earlier, Ellen's small group is very supportive of Christian mind development. By their choice of discussion and study topics, books and activities (for example, enrolling in a ten-week course together), a great deal can be accomplished. And although the downtown Christian businessmen's group is an enclave of male chauvinism and uncritical Thank-God-my-business-is-booming-since-I-converted-and-stopped-drinking testimonials, Ellen has found a group of four other business leaders near her office who meet with her for lunch and discussion once a week.

Stan needs to be careful not to hide himself completely in his work, fascinating as he finds it! His two anti-intellectual Christian roommates ought not to be avoided, nor scorned. Instead, Stan could suggest a weekly house Bible study and merely note the frequency with which matters of mind and work are brought up. It is impossible for any true Bible lover to retain a compartmentalized life after an honest study of Scripture. There simply are no exception clauses in any part of the Bible.

Stan can never say, "Jesus is Lord of my life except for my engineering and my university studies." It often takes a lot of patience to overcome comfortable, deeply ingrained, self-justifying viewpoints. But most evangelicals and fundamentalists really are committed to the authority of Jesus and Scripture, and with time and careful study they will bend to this authority.

Stan also should work on his schedule, priorities and on building a network of Christian mind colleagues. He should join the American Scientific Affiliation and start participating in their activities. He has made some preliminary moves to find other Christians in Silicon Valley for a small fellowship and study group. As a single man with a good paycheck, Stan has adequate time and money to become a part-time theological student, build a good library and put in ten or more hours per week on his Christian growth.

Bill is already part of the network of the Christian Medical Society (CMS), and the chances are excellent that wherever he takes a job as a physician he will quickly find other CMS members in a local chapter. Bill completed a year of full-time Christian integrative studies and is thus a few steps ahead of our other friends in this quest. However, developing a Christian mind is a lifelong adventure, and Bill knows he has much to learn. Bill needs to assume some leadership in assisting medical students and colleagues in their own journeys toward Christian minds. Predictably, the time pressures on a doctor (especially one with a young family) will be one of Bill's greatest challenges. By doubling up on certain activities (like teaching a Sunday-school class on the same subject he is researching for a CMS Journal article), Bill will best be able to continue growing in a sane way!

Debbie's university strategy has already been reviewed. Since she has a warm and deep relationship with her family and church, it is enough to suggest that she try to contribute what she is learning to both of those communities. That is, Debbie could volunteer to lead a Sunday-school class for high-school students on parts of the Bible she is studying (in her quest to study all sixty-six books!). She might help lead a church retreat on "The Christian Mind" or "Discipleship on the Job." By teaching in this way she will be reinforcing what she is learning, and she will also be discovering whether she is really gifted and called to teach.

These are by no means exhaustive or comprehensive strategies, even for our four friends. However, they exemplify concrete ways in which busy, diverse Christian disciples can work at bringing their minds and lives more fully under the lordship of Jesus Christ.

For Reflection and Discussion

1. What aspects of your schedule can be, and need to be, rearranged to make developing a Christian mind more of a priority?

2. Would the strategy for personal study described in this chapter work for you? What have been your experiences previously with any parts of it, like systematic Bible study? Redesign any parts of it so that it will best challenge *you*.

3. What institutional support can you take advantage of? Schools, church groups, professional organizations?

Notes

[1] John A. Bernbaum and Simon M. Steer, *Why Work?* (Grand Rapids, Mich.: Baker, 1986), and Brian J. Walsh and J. Richard Middleton, *The Transforming Vision* (Downers Grove, Ill.: InterVarsity Press, 1984), both have helpful lists of books, journals and vocational associations in many different fields.

[2] I'm not knocking the value of such meetings, as far as they go. But the Word of God invites us to reflect on the totality of our work and life, not just the critical (and wonderful) moment of new birth.

[3] The new InterVarsity Marketplace Ministry division is one of the best things to happen to campus ministry in this century!

[4] "Can Seminaries Adapt to the Student of the '80s?" *Christianity Today,* February 7, 1986, p. 39.

GRADUATION
REQUIREMENTS:
WHAT IT TAKES TO
•SALT THE EARTH•
9

It would be very difficult for us to find convincing texts for a biblical theology of conformism. The biblical injunctions to penetrate the world always turn out to have *transforming* objectives. Whatever conformity and accommodation are required by our efforts to be fully incarnate in the world are always gu·ded and limited by love and by a determination to introduce the will of God which is specific, unique and incommensurable with fallen reality.

So why is it that we see so little nonconformity, so much earth and so little salt?[1] Given the numerical strength of Christianity as indicated in opinion polls and church membership statistics, one would expect to see Christians having a vigorous impact on the culture. My observation is that there is plenty of good will and good faith in the Christian community. I do not think that Christians are deliberately ineffective and inconsequential in their presence in the world!

Part of the reason for our conformism is ignorance of certain very prominent biblical themes. "You must not live according to the customs of the nations. . . . I am the LORD your God, who has set you apart from the nations. . . . You are to be holy to me because I, the LORD, am holy, and I have set you apart from the nations to be my own" (Lev 20:23-24, 26). These same themes from the Old Testament story of Israel are applied to the Christian church in the New Testament: "Just as he who called you is holy, so be holy in all you do; for it is written: 'Be holy, because I am holy.'. . . Live . . . as strangers here in reverent fear" (1 Pet 1:15-17). Jesus himself gave classic expression to our calling to be "in" the world but not "of" the world (Jn 17). Paul called Christians to "not conform any longer to the pattern of this world, but be transformed by the renewing of your mind" (Rom 12:2).

This is not a call for maladjustment or eccentricity for its own sake! Holy nonconformism is a difference defined by God's difference with the world. Be holy *just as* God is holy. Be in, but not of, the world *just as* Jesus was in but not of this world. This transformation will mean that we are the salt and light of the world around us (Mt 5:13-16). As salt we preserve the world in a certain sense; we retard its decay (this was the ancient use of salt implied in Jesus' statement). As light we illuminate situations and their meaning; we bring life and freedom, truth and visible good works. Given the decay of American society, it hardly seems that Christians are getting the job done. What kind of efforts will make a difference?

My study of Scripture and observations of many Christians who have made a difference lead me to conclude that there are five elements in the composition of Christian salt. *The Opening of the Christian Mind* is addressed to a large segment of the Christian community: those who are studying in the universities of our time and those working at thoughtful discipleship, Monday through Sunday, in the marketplace. The five characteristics of Christian salt apply everywhere in the Christian church, but they have special relevance for those seeking Christian minds.

Conviction

The first element is *the conviction that Jesus Christ is Lord of the whole of life*—my life, the life of the world. Jesus is Lord not just of the inner life, afterlife, family life and church life, but of intellectual life, political life—all domains. This is an intellectual affirmation—an idea we believe to be true. But more than that it must be a conviction that grips us personally in heart and mind and brings dedicated commitment of our life and energy.

We have heard the Great Command given by Jesus: "Love the Lord your God with all your heart and with all your soul and with all your strength and with all your mind" (Lk 10:27). Pretty all-inclusive! "Take captive every thought to make it obedient to Christ" (2 Cor 10:5). "Live a life worthy of the Lord and . . . please him in every way" (Col 1:10). "Whatever you do, whether in word or deed, do it all in the name of the Lord" (Col 3:17). The Old Testament demonstrates God's holistic claim in its laws and regulations about dress, food, agriculture, the calendar, political order, business and so much else. The New Testament loosens the specifics of these regulations but insists that all of these areas remain under God's rule. Hence, family, money, justice and other areas are the subject of large parts of New Testament teaching. There is no escaping this unanimous thrust of the Bible in favor of the conviction that Jesus is Lord of all.

Francis Schaeffer, the late author and founder/leader of the L'Abri Fellowship, is a great example of someone consumed by this conviction. His brash attempts to reinterpret all of Western civilization, art, film, philosophy, politics and so on, grew out of intense conviction. E. F. Schumacher, the late British economist and author of *Small Is Beautiful: Economics as if People Mattered,* insisted on bringing God into a domain which ruthlessly excluded him. Dr. Charles Tucker, one of my students who now practices medicine, carried out a bold study of his profession's approach to money and patient fees in light of Scripture. Debra Jarvis, another student, drew together her work as a humorous novelist with her understanding of the role of humor in Scripture.

Jesus is Lord of Ellen's banking, Bill's medicine, Stan's high tech and

Debbie's career decision between teaching and law. Passionately believing that is the beginning point.

If we don't have this conviction: no salt!

Courage

I find that actually a fairly large percentage of Christians do hold this conviction. But by itself, it is not enough. For we need, secondly, *the courage to act on our conviction that Jesus is Lord of all.* Even the pagan Greek philosophers recognized courage as one of the cardinal virtues. Courage, or fortitude, meant literally the readiness to fall in battle. Guts, reckless, risky faith in God: If we don't have a dose of this our conviction is for naught.

"Have I not commanded you? Be strong and courageous. Do not be terrified; do not be discouraged, for the LORD your God will be with you wherever you go" (Josh 1:9). For us as for Joshua the source of courage is obedience to the command of God and confidence that the living God is with us at every moment and will not abandon us. Think of David standing up to Goliath, or Abraham leaving home not knowing where he was going (Heb 11:8). Think of Peter stepping out of the boat onto the ocean in the dark! (Matt 14:29). Hebrews 11 gives a long list of courageous examples of the faithful. The Bible calls for courage from cover to cover.

Eric Liddell, the British runner whose story was told in the film *Chariots of Fire*, showed remarkable courage in declining to race on Sunday, choosing to bear the anger of his teammates and nation and forego Olympic glory if necessary. To many of us, Senator Mark Hatfield exemplifies great courage as he stands up for what he believes is right—and continually experiences hostility from right and left, Republican and Democrat, and even his fellow evangelicals more often than not. George Miller, a student at New College Berkeley a few years ago, was offered a job with the Immigration Service at a time when he dearly wanted a job in his field of criminal justice. But after an extensive study of biblical teaching on how the people of God are to treat the stranger coming in their midst, George had the courage to turn it down. (He is now thriving as a probation officer in Alaska!)

God will walk with Ellen in the hallways and boardrooms of her bank, with Stan in his computer center, with Bill in his operating room and clinic, and with Debbie in her classroom. Knowing that God walks with us is the source of our courage to speak and act on our conviction that Jesus is Lord.

No courage, no salt!

Creativity

Some of us have conviction and courage, but that is not enough either. We are like divers up on the high board ready to take the leap—but we don't know how! We are determined to dive off, not climb back down the ladder, but will anything happen except that we make laughingstocks of ourselves and maybe get hurt? What we desperately need is an idea how to dive off. As Christians we must have the *creativity to discern or invent ways of being faithful to our convictions.*

The Bible demonstrates this creative introduction of new options all the time. The Jubilee Year preserved both free enterprise and social welfare in Israel's economy (Lev 25). Gideon defeated the Midianites with trumpets, torches and jars, without firing a shot (Judg 7). Creativity is found especially in Jesus' death and resurrection. After the resurrection *nothing* is impossible, no situation is impenetrable. Nothing in this world is so certain and closed as death and the grave; but Jesus broke through to new life. We must never give up looking for creative alternatives in apparently closed situations.

Gene Thomas, a Boulder, Colorado, businessman, created laundry and house-painting businesses to provide jobs and psychological health to people regarded as hopeless, incurable, unemployable losers in his city. The city gave up; Gene didn't. The Christian Legal Society pioneered Christian Conciliation Centers as a creative response to Christians' need for alternative methods of resolving conflicts outside of the courtroom. McGhee Avenue Baptist Church, an urban congregation in Berkeley, started its own credit union to provide better savings and loan services for its parishioners than the regular banks would. E. F. Schumacher's Scott Bader Corporation in England limited its number of employees in order to maintain personal relations, contributed a regular percentage of its profits to community improvements around the factory, and included all employees in a profit-sharing system that motivated them to better work and company loyalty.

The truly salty Christians I have known in business, politics, education and other areas have refused to be limited to the options of the world around them. They have rejected realism, fatalism, pessimism and conformism. They have been open-grave people, walk-on-water people, who prayed and worked until creative new options opened up. No matter how novel the challenge—or how fixed and immovable the obstacles—Ellen, Bill, Stan and Debbie can know from Scripture and Christian history that a creative alternative will appear if they keep working and looking for it.

Without this creativity, the salt has no saltiness.

Competence

Conviction + courage + creativity doesn't quite add up to Christian salt yet. We must show *competence in carrying out our creative alternatives*. I have discussed this need for excellence in an earlier section on professional expertise but it applies across the board. Say you have the conviction and courage and then a creative idea: I'll write a critique of the rise and fall of Western civilization from a Christian point of view. Great idea! But then if it is shot through with errors of fact and interpretation—incompetently done—we are no better off afterwards than before!

Biblically, the pattern is set when God's creation is designated "very good." And the pattern ends for us, we hope, with "Well done, good and faithful servant" (Mt 25:21). The scandal and offense of Christianity is the cross (1 Cor 1:23). The scandal should never be our incompetence.

The excellence and competence to which I refer is measured by (a) God's standards insofar as we can know them (including truthfulness, sacrificial love, joy, humility), (b) our own gifts, abilities and circumstances (2 Cor 8:11-12 speaks specifically about financial gifts, but it reflects a broad biblical theme), and only last in priority (c) the prevailing standards in our field. Thus, I don't think this means we all need to be geniuses and stars, bowling people over with our perfection and excellence! But we must aim as high as possible for the glory of God. Reasonable competence is what we need.

Handel's *Messiah* is sung even by pagans every year because it is so excellent! *Chariots of Fire* won the Academy Award for Best Picture because it is excellent. Most Christian music and film is rejected or neglected by our culture not because of prejudice against the cross but because the products are second-rate. The Edwin Hawkins Singers' recording of "O Happy Day" was the number-one hit on all the charts in the early seventies because it was a hot, great piece of musical performance. "O Happy Day! When Jesus washed my sins away!" was played *everywhere* for a while. So much for prejudice against Christian music. There is a reason why some popular Christian authors' works are ignored by the world: their books aren't very good.

I do not deny that there are cases of anti-Christian prejudice in all sectors of our society. But I have found that in my own history and in other cases I observe, it is usually due to incompetence on the part of those rejected. Fortunately, Ellen, Stan, Bill and Debbie are all committed to excellence and competence in their faith and life. But the pressures of time will always put our standards of excellence at risk.

Without a minimum of competence, our salt is incomplete and ineffective.

Community

We can have conviction, courage, creativity and competence—and still fail to salt the earth. We must have the *community to support and correct our discipleship in the world.* This seems so obvious, but our practice is so frequently individualistic. Christian discipleship is not for Lone Rangers (though in all fairness, even the masked man had Tonto as his sidekick). We must resist the individualism of our culture and cultivate deep and strong relationships with others. The challenges we face are formidable; without community they become impossible.

Remember Jesus' promise. "For where two or three come together in my name, there am I with them" (Mt 18:20). Paul says, "Do not think of yourself more highly than you ought," and proceeds to discuss the interdependence of the members of the body of Christ (Rom 12:3-8). The idea of peoplehood is also strong in the Old Testament, beginning with the declaration that "It is not good for the man to be alone" (Gen 2:18).

Our experience and practice of community takes many shapes, from family and friendship to small groups to the church to Christian professional groups. The form is flexible and varied, but somehow it has to be there. Community interaction clarifies and then reinforces our convictions. Community shores up our courage. There is strength in numbers. Community is crucial to creativity. What we need are Christian brain trusts—Christian gatherings and groups to brainstorm new possibilities for our job or for evangelism. Most of us know well the creative ferment of brainstorming in which many great ideas are generated. Community means we share with each other what we know, providing each other with solutions or the provocation to a solution. Community assists competence because we can catch each other's errors, toughen each other's arguments, shore up any weaknesses we might have missed alone.

Community helps us to discern what to do, how to do it and when. But community also stands by while we do it, supporting us, assisting us, catching if we fall. I'm better able to dive off the board if I know you will fish me out in a pinch. Community is all these things, and not just because of principles of group dynamics! Rather it is the dwelling place of the Spirit of God. God's Holy Spirit works in special ways through the body of Christ.

As we have seen earlier, Stan is our most vulnerable friend on this score. He needs to move aggressively to build a small community of support. Ellen's family and small group, Bill's Christian Medical Society chapter and Debbie's InterVarsity chapter are providing them with this kind of community in important ways.

Without a basic community, our Christian mind and our discipleship are imperilled.

If these five components are present—conviction, courage, creativity, competence and community—Christian salt is formed as surely as if sodium and chloride were combined to make the NaCl we put on our food.

Much of this book feeds the discussion on creativity and competence. As I have tried to stress throughout this study, developing a Christian mind is in fact a command of God which we are bound to obey. But God always makes a way, and gives us the tools and strength to obey his commands. In fact, he gives us more than we need for minimal compliance! He opens doors leading to new vistas we never imagined existed. The adventure completely swallows up the obligation. We find ourselves drawn, though we might have started out driven.

I am certain that if you prayerfully adopt the conviction outlined in the first chapter, prayerfully muster the courage to move out on the strategies suggested in the eighth chapter, you will before long begin experiencing the marks of a Christian mind described in chapter four. You will be gratified—and more importantly, God will be glorified.

Inevitably, a great deal of work has been added to our busy agendas. But we must remember that the Christian life, including our quest for a Christian mind, is in the end a gracious gift from God. It is a possession we are invited to enter, more fundamentally than a sort of building to be erected in our own strength.

We need to be aggressive about attempting great things for God. But this is always qualified by the peaceful invitation to expect great things from God. We will need to exert ourselves in the Christian life. But the burden should not be heavy, for we do not carry the responsibility for empowering ourselves. In our own flesh, our bodies as well as our minds and spirits will soon grow weary. But in the adventure of the Christian mind, as in all aspects of the Christian life, "those who hope in the LORD will renew their strength. They will soar on wings like eagles; they will run and not grow weary, they will walk and not be faint" (Is 40:31). If we pursue a Christian mind we are taking on a great task for our Lord.

If it becomes a toilsome burden at any time, we must stop for a moment and ask God to refill us with the love, joy, peace and patience that can only come from his Spirit.

For Reflection and Discussion

1. Have you ever done anything notably courageous in your life? How did you feel? What were the costs, the benefits?

2. How creative are you? How creative do you trust God is? How have you experienced his creativity in working out seemingly impossible situations, or in answering prayers in unimaginable ways?

3. How do you assess the issue of competence in the Christian community and its activities in the world? Is there as much incompetence as this chapter suggests? What have you observed? What are your standards?

Notes

[1]A brilliant study of this problem on a larger scale is Jacques Ellul, *The Subversion of Christianity* (Grand Rapids, Mich.: Eerdmans, 1986).

Bibliography

Adeney, Bernard T., "Work: Necessity, Vocation and Servanthood," *Radix Magazine,* Jan.-Feb. 1984, pp. 16-17.

Banks, Robert. *All the Business of Life: Bringing Theology Down to Earth.* Sutherland, Australia: Albatross, 1987.

──────. *The Tyranny of Time.* Downers Grove, Ill.: InterVarsity Press, 1984.

Barclay, Oliver R. *The Intellect and Beyond.* Grand Rapids: Zondervan, 1985.

Bellah, Robert N. "Civil Religion in America." In *Religion in America,* edited by W. G. McLoughlin and Robert Bellah. Boston: Houghton Mifflin, 1968, pp. 3-23.

Bellah, Robert N. et al. *Habits of the Heart: Individualism and Commitment in American Life.* Berkeley: University of California Press, 1985.

Bernbaum, John A., and Simon M. Steer. *Why Work? Careers and Employment in Biblical Perspective.* Grand Rapids: Baker Book House, 1986.

Blamires, Harry. *The Christian Mind: How Should A Christian Think?* London: SPCK, 1963; Ann Arbor: Servant Books, 1978.

Bloom, Allan. *The Closing of the American Mind.* New York: Simon and Schuster, 1987.

Christianity Today. "Can Seminaries Adapt to the Student of the '80s?" February 7, 1986, pp. 35-40.

Cullman, Oscar. *Christ and Time.* Philadelphia: Westminster Press, 1952.

Dyrness, William A. *Themes in Old Testament Theology.* Downers Grove, Ill.: InterVarsity Press, 1979.

Eller, Vernard. *Christian Anarchy: Jesus' Primacy Over the Powers.* Grand Rapids: Eerdmans, 1987.

Ellul, Jacques. *Money and Power.* Downers Grove, Ill.: InterVarsity Press, 1984.

——————. *The New Demons.* New York: Seabury Press, 1975.

——————. *The Presence of the Kingdom.* New York: Seabury Press, 1970.

——————. *The Subversion of Christianity.* Grand Rapids: Eerdmans, 1986.

——————. *The Technological Society.* New York: Vintage, 1964.

Foster, Richard J. *Celebration of Discipline: The Path to Spiritual Growth.* San Francisco: Harper & Row, 1978.

Gill, David W. *Peter the Rock: Extraordinary Insights from an Ordinary Man.* Downers Grove, Ill.: InterVarsity Press, 1986.

——————. "Secularism." In *Evangelical Dictionary of Theology,* edited by Walter A. Elwell. Grand Rapids: Baker, 1984, pp. 996-97.

——————. *The Word of God in the Ethics of Jacques Ellul.* ATLA Monograph No. 20. Metuchen, N.J.: Scarecrow Press, 1984.

Green, Joel B. *How to Read Prophecy.* Downers Grove, Ill.: InterVarsity Press, 1984.

——————. *How to Read the Gospels and Acts.* Downers Grove, Ill.: InterVarsity Press, 1987.

Gustafson, James M. "The University as a Community of Moral Discourse." *Journal of Religion* 53 (1973): 397-409.

Hauerwas, Stanley. *A Community of Character.* South Bend: Notre Dame, 1981.

Hirsch, E. D., Jr. *Cultural Literacy: What Every American Needs to Know.*

Boston: Houghton Mifflin, 1987.

Holmes, Arthur F. *Contours of a World View*. Grand Rapids: Eerdmans, 1983.

——————. *The Idea of a Christian College*. Grand Rapids: Eerdmans, 1975.

——————, ed. *The Making of a Christian Mind: A Christian World View and the Academic Enterprise*. Downers Grove, Ill.: InterVarsity Press, 1985.

Illich, Ivan. *Celebration of Awareness: A Call for Institutional Revolution*. New York: Doubleday Anchor, 1970.

——————. *Deschooling Society*. New York: Harper & Row, 1970.

——————. *Tools for Conviviality*. New York: Harper & Row, 1973.

——————. *Toward a History of Needs*. New York: Pantheon Books, 1977.

Kerr, Clark. *The Uses of the University*. 3rd ed. Cambridge, Mass.: Harvard University, 1982.

Lasch, Christopher. *The Culture of Narcissism*. New York: Norton, 1978.

Malik, Charles Habib. *A Christian Critique of the University*. Downers Grove, Ill.: InterVarsity Press, 1982.

Monsma, Stephen V., ed. *Responsible Technology*. Grand Rapids: Eerdmans, 1986.

Newman, John Henry Cardinal. *The Idea of a University*, Rev. ed., 1873. New York: Doubleday Image, 1959.

Pieper, Josef. *Leisure: The Basis of Culture*. New York: Mentor, 1952, 1963.

Pippert, Rebecca Manley. *Out of the Saltshaker*. Downers Grove, Ill.: InterVarsity Press, 1979.

Schumacher, E. F. *Small Is Beautiful: Economics as if People Mattered*. New York: Harper & Row, 1976.

Sloan, Douglas. "The Teaching of Ethics in the American Undergraduate Curriculum, 1876-1976." In *Ethics Teaching in Higher Education*, edited by Daniel Callahan and Sissela Bok, pp. 1-57. Hastings-on-Hudson, N.Y.: The Hastings Center, 1980.

Snyder, Howard. *The Problem of Wineskins*. Downers Grove, Ill.: InterVarsity Press, 1975.

Stadtman, Verne A. *The University of California, 1868-1968.* New York: McGraw-Hill, 1970.

Walsh, Brian J. and J. Richard Middleton. *The Transforming Vision: Shaping a Christian World View.* Downers Grove, Ill.: InterVarsity Press, 1984.

Yoder, John Howard. *The Politics of Jesus.* Grand Rapids: Eerdmans, 1972.